Understanding
World History

The Rise of
the Nazis

Hal Marcovitz

Bruno Leone
Series Consultant

ReferencePoint
Press®

San Diego, CA

© 2015 ReferencePoint Press, Inc.
Printed in the United States

For more information, contact:
ReferencePoint Press, Inc.
PO Box 27779
San Diego, CA 92198
www.ReferencePointPress.com

LIBRARY OF CONGRESS CATALOGING-IN-PUBLICATION DATA

Marcovitz, Hal.
  The rise of the Nazis / by Hal Marcovitz.
     pages cm. -- (Understanding world history series)
  Includes bibliographical references and index.
  ISBN-13: 978-1-60152-654-0 (hardback)
  ISBN-10: 1-60152-654-7 (hardback)
  1. National socialism--Juvenile literature. 2. Germany--History--1918-1933--Juvenile literature.
  3. Germany--History--1933-1945--Juvenile literature. 4. Hitler, Adolf, 1889-1945--Juvenile
  literature. 5. Holocaust, Jewish (1939-1945)--Juvenile literature. I. Title.
  DD256.5.M334 2015
  943.086--dc23
                                                                              2013044393

Contents

Foreword

When the Puritans first emigrated from England to America in 1630, they believed that their journey was blessed by a covenant between themselves and God. By the terms of that covenant they agreed to establish a community in the New World dedicated to what they believed was the true Christian faith. God, in turn, would reward their fidelity by making certain that they and their descendants would always experience his protection and enjoy material prosperity. Moreover, the Lord guaranteed that their land would be seen as a shining beacon—or in their words, a "city upon a hill"—that the rest of the world would view with admiration and respect. By embracing this notion that God could and would shower his favor and special blessings upon them, the Puritans were adopting the providential philosophy of history—meaning that history is the unfolding of a plan established or guided by a higher intelligence.

The concept of intercession by a divine power is only one of many explanations of the driving forces of world history. Historians and philosophers alike have subscribed to numerous other ideas. For example, the ancient Greeks and Romans argued that history is cyclical. Nations and civilizations, according to these ancients of the Western world, rise and fall in unpredictable cycles; the only certainty is that these cycles will persist throughout an endless future. The German historian Oswald Spengler (1880–1936) echoed the ancients to some degree in his controversial study *The Decline of the West*. Spengler asserted that all civilizations inevitably pass through stages comparable to the life span of a person: childhood, youth, adulthood, old age, and, eventually, death. As the title of his work implies, Western civilization is currently entering its final stage.

Joining those who see purpose and direction in history are thinkers who completely reject the idea of meaning or certainty. Rather, they reason that since there are far too many random and unseen factors at work on the earth, historians would be unwise to endorse historical predictability of any type. Warfare (both nuclear and conventional), plagues, earthquakes, tsunamis, meteor showers, and other catastrophic world-changing events have loomed large throughout history and prehistory. In his essay "A Free Man's Worship," philosopher and mathematician Bertrand Russell (1872–1970) supported this argument, which many refer to as the nihilist or chaos theory of history. According to Russell, history follows no preordained path. Rather, the earth itself and all life on earth resulted from, as Russell describes it, an "accidental collocation of atoms." Based on this premise, he pessimistically concluded that all human achievement will eventually be "buried beneath the debris of a universe in ruins."

Whether history does or does not have an underlying purpose, historians, journalists, and countless others have nonetheless left behind a record of human activity tracing back nearly 6,000 years. From the dawn of the great ancient Near Eastern civilizations of Mesopotamia and Egypt to the modern economic and military behemoths China and the United States, humanity's deeds and misdeeds have been and continue to be monitored and recorded. The distinguished British scholar Arnold Toynbee (1889–1975), in his widely acclaimed twelve-volume work entitled *A Study of History,* studied twenty-one different civilizations that have passed through history's pages. He noted with certainty that others would follow.

In the final analysis, the academic and journalistic worlds mostly regard history as a record and explanation of past events. From a more practical perspective, history represents a sequence of building blocks—cultural, technological, military, and political—ready to be utilized and enhanced or maligned and perverted by the present. What that means is that all societies—whether advanced civilizations or preliterate tribal cultures—leave a legacy for succeeding generations to either embrace or disregard.

Recognizing the richness and fullness of history, the ReferencePoint Press Understanding World History series fosters an evaluation and interpretation of history and its influence on later generations. Each volume in the series approaches its subject chronologically and topically, with specific focus on nations, periods, or pivotal events. Primary and secondary source quotations are included, along with complete source notes and suggestions for further research.

Moreover, the series reflects the truism that the key to understanding the present frequently lies in the past. With that in mind, each series title concludes with a legacy chapter that highlights the bonds between past and present and, more important, demonstrates that world history is a continuum of peoples and ideas, sometimes hidden but there nonetheless, waiting to be discovered by those who choose to look.

1889
Adolf Hitler is born on April 20 in the town of Braunau am Inn, Austria.

1919
Hitler attends a meeting of the German Workers' Party and finds himself enthralled by the group's dedication to nationalism, German exceptionalism, and racist principles.

1914
On July 29, Austrian troops lay siege to the Serbian capital of Belgrade, touching off World War I; Hitler enlists in the German army and serves bravely, winning two decorations.

1900   **1910**   **1920**

1918
The German government signs the armistice, agreeing to withdraw its troops and end the war; German troops return home, many believing they did not lose the war but were withdrawn by politicians too weak to continue the battle.

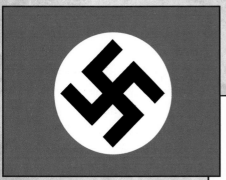

1920
On February 20, now head of propaganda for the German Workers' Party, Hitler stages the party's first major event; two thousand people attend a four-hour rally at a Munich beer hall.

1921
In July Hitler's adversaries in what is now known as the Nazi Party attempt to forge a merger with a similar group; Hitler defeats the merger and solidifies his position as Nazi führer.

1923
On November 8, Hitler stages the Beer Hall Putsch, an attempt to take over the Bavarian government. The putsch fails; Hitler is arrested and imprisoned.

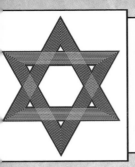

1925
Mein Kampf is published; the book lays out Hitler's vision for European domination as well as his hatred for Jews, Slavs, Communists, and other groups.

1938
On September 22, German troops cross into Czechoslovakia to reclaim the Sudetenland for Germany; British prime minister Neville Chamberlain is accused of appeasing Hitler by not opposing the invasion.

1941
On December 11, four days after the Japanese attack on Pearl Harbor in Hawaii, Germany declares war on the United States.

1928
Nazi candidates compete for the first time in German national elections; the party fairs dismally, winning just 3 percent of the vote and 12 seats in the 491-seat Reichstag.

1944
Allied troops land in Normandy, France, on June 6, commencing the invasion of the European continent that would lead to the defeat of Germany.

1934
Hitler stages the Night of the Long Knives on June 30, murdering some four hundred of his political adversaries, including Ernst Röhm, the thuggish head of the Sturmabteilung.

1930 **1935** **1940** **1945**

1933
Hitler is named chancellor by President Paul von Hindenburg on January 20.

1939
German troops invade Poland on September 1, touching off World War II.

1945
Hitler—hiding in his underground bunker in Berlin—commits suicide on April 30 as Russian troops close in.

1932
The Nazis become the dominant party in the Reichstag, polling 14 million votes and capturing 230 seats.

1930
As economic depression engulfs Germany, many voters turn a friendly ear toward the Nazi message of nationalism and German exceptionalism, awarding Nazi candidates 107 seats in the Reichstag.

The Defining Characteristics of Nazism's Rise

In the years following World War I, Germans found themselves living in a land of turmoil. Defeated in what was known then as the Great War, the nation was hit by massive unemployment and inflation—the increasing cost of consumer goods. Vast numbers of Germans were mired in poverty. Searching for hope and a path to prosperity, many Germans found themselves awed by the enormous personal magnetism of a single man who proved himself a master of propaganda. Adolf Hitler won over the German people by promising to restore Germany's honor and, moreover, to install Germany as the ruler of all European nations. And in electing to follow Hitler, the German people also embraced the racist notions of the movement he helped create: Nationalsozialismus, meaning "National Socialism," or "Nazism," for short.

The Nazis were fiercely nationalistic, believing in the supremacy of the German people. They never accepted the defeat of the German army, believing their military leaders and politicians had caved in to internal squabbling and pressure to bring the conflict to a close.

This anger came to a boil on November 8, 1923, when Hitler, the leader of the Nazis, waged a campaign to take over the government. His campaign started in the city of Munich, where Gustav von Kahr, the Bavarian prime minister, intended to address a group of businessmen at a beer hall. Hitler was accompanied by four hundred paramilitary thugs, members of a private army known as the Sturmabteilung (SA), or "Storm Section." As SA members held Kahr at gunpoint, Hitler took the podium and declared, "A new national government will be named this very day here in Munich!"[1]

Chaos ensued in the city as the SA attempted to seize control of government offices. The next morning Hitler led a parade of three thousand armed SA troops into the center of Munich. They were met by German army troops who opened fire. Sixteen Nazis died while dozens more were wounded. Hitler and other leaders of what became known as the Beer Hall Putsch (*putsch* is a German word for "coup") were arrested. Four months later Hitler was convicted of treason and sentenced to five years in prison.

Hitler's Struggle

Hitler served only a fraction of his sentence; he was paroled after a mere nine months. Hitler made good use of his time behind bars; during his imprisonment he wrote a book laying out his vision for Germany. Journalist William L. Shirer, who covered the rise of Hitler and the Nazis during the 1920s and 1930s, contends that,

> for whatever other accusations can be made against Adolf Hitler, no one can accuse him of not putting down in writing exactly the kind of Germany he intended to make if he ever came to power and the kind of world he meant to create by armed German conquest. The blueprint . . . of the barbaric New Order which Hitler inflicted on conquered Europe in the triumphant years between 1939 and 1945 is set down in all its appalling crudity at great length and in detail between the covers of this revealing book.[2]

The book, titled *Mein Kampf (My Struggle)*, focuses on Hitler's racist philosophy, establishing higher and lower orders of humans. According to Hitler, those of Germanic—or Aryan—ancestry, having blond hair, fair skin, and blue eyes, are of the highest order. Germans, Hitler asserts, are members of a master race.

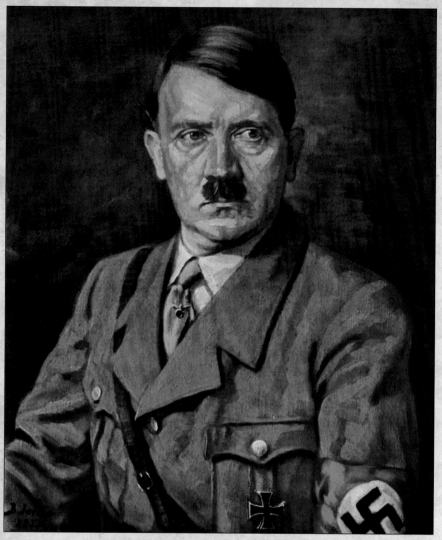

In the wake of Germany's demoralizing defeat in World War I, Adolf Hitler promised to restore his country's honor and prosperity. He also set a course for German dominance over neighboring countries and world affairs.

All others belong to lesser forms of humanity: what he called the *Untermenschen,* or "racially inferior." Among the *Untermenschen* are the Slavic peoples—Czechs, Poles, Russians, and others from eastern Europe. Hitler asserted, "[Nazism] by no means believes in equality of the races, but along with their difference it recognizes their higher or lesser value and feels itself obligated, through this knowledge, to promote the victory of the better and stronger, and demand the subordination of the inferior and weaker in accordance with the eternal will that dominates this universe."[3]

Hatred of the Jews

Hitler reserved his most venomous prose for Jews, believing them to be racially inferior. He also believed Jews were using their money and influence to keep the German people from fulfilling their potential. "The Aryan understands labor as the foundation for preservation of the people's community," Hitler claimed. "The Jew sees it as the means to exploit other peoples."[4]

To counter the affliction of racial impurity by Slavs, Jews, and others, Hitler proposed a bold vision: Germany should rebuild its army and expand its borders, encompassing the entirety of Europe. In effect, Hitler was proposing a new war against the nations of Europe and, following German conquest, the obliteration or enslavement of millions of Slavs, Jews, and others.

Hitler's message of hate found traction among destitute Germans looking for scapegoats to blame for the inflation, unemployment, and poverty that gripped their lives. *Mein Kampf* was published in 1925, helping to spread Hitler's message throughout Germany. By the 1930s only the Bible was outselling *Mein Kampf* in Germany. Shirer finds it chilling that so many millions of Germans failed to see the depravity of the book's message—a "grotesque hodgepodge concocted by a half-baked, uneducated neurotic."[5] Equally troubling is that they were so willing to follow its author down a path that would lead to the loss of tens of millions of lives, the destruction of their country, and one of the darkest eras in the history of human civilization.

Chapter 1

What Conditions Led to the Rise of the Nazis?

By the middle of the nineteenth century, most European countries had established their borders and adopted national identities, cultures, and common languages—but that was not the case in Germany. The German people lived in smaller kingdoms and principalities, with names such as Bohemia, Saxony, Pomerania, Lorraine, and Franconia. Over the years many German leaders had called for the unification of the German peoples into a single nation, but the individual monarchs who held power had insisted on maintaining their dominions.

The most powerful of these German states was Prussia, led by a monarch, Wilhelm I, who ascended the throne in 1861. Serving as prime minister under Wilhelm was a wily and savvy prince named Otto von Bismarck. Bismarck called for a unified Germany but wanted to ensure that Prussia would emerge as the dominant force in the unified state. Bismarck took the first steps toward unification by overseeing a massive industrialization and militarization of Prussia and by using Prussia's military might to pressure smaller German states into forming diplomatic alliances.

In 1870 Prussia waged war against France. Bismarck orchestrated a minor dispute over the Spanish throne into a major insult against the French, provoking them into declaring war. He rallied the other German states into a coalition to fight against the French. Led by the superior Prussian army, the German states defeated the French within a year. In 1871, as part of the treaty that ended the Franco-Prussian War, Wilhelm accepted the crown as emperor—or kaiser—of a unified Germany. Representatives were elected to a single parliament, known as the Reichstag, a German word that translates to "diet (or legislature) of the realm." In reality, though, the Reichstag held little power, for Wilhelm and Bismarck remained the true authority in the new Germany.

German Exceptionalism

As Bismarck unified Germany, a second powerful state also emerged in Europe: Austria-Hungary. The nation had been created in 1867, replacing what formerly had been known as the Austrian Empire. Ruled by the Habsburg monarchy, Austria held dominion over several lands with large Slavic populations, including Hungary. As opposition to Habsburg rule grew in Hungary, Emperor Franz Joseph forged a compromise, establishing a dual monarchy. Franz Joseph remained emperor under the compromise, but Hungarian nobles would be granted authority to rule over their dominions. Nevertheless, under the dual monarchy, Hungarians found themselves ruled by an emperor who spoke German and maintained a close political relationship with German leaders.

Across Europe, the late 1800s and early 1900s reflected a period of great change and upheaval as some nations embraced democracy and others clung to their monarchies. In the streets of European capitals, Communists and their violence-prone cohorts, known as anarchists, hatched plots against ruling authorities. Many political ideologies were debated in the taverns and beer halls of European cities. Even in Germany, a nation enjoying the fruits of the Industrial Revolution as well as its emergence as a dominant military and political power on the European continent, dissidents developed their ideologies and drew their plans.

Many Germans were drawn to the writings of Johann Gottlieb Fichte, an early nineteenth-century philosopher who was among the first to propose the notion of German nationalism. Fichte argued that Germans should come together as part of a common nation and, moreover, sacrifice their wealth and even their lives in the cause of a unified German state. Fichte also proposed the notion of German exceptionalism—meaning that Germans were, by their nature, superior to the other nationalities that populated the European continent. "[Among] all modern peoples, it is you in whom the seed of human perfection most decidedly lies and to whom the lead in its development is assigned," Fichte wrote in a message to the German people in 1807. "If you perish . . . then all the hopes of the entire human race for salvation from the depths of its miseries perish

The unification of Germany was accomplished in 1871 by Prussian monarch Wilhelm I (left) and his prime minister Otto von Bismarck (right). Although a parliament was created and its members elected, Wilhelm and Bismarck held full authority over the new Germany.

with you. . . . If you sink, all humanity sinks with you, without hope of future restoration."[6]

Another writer, the Austrian Georg Ritter von Schönerer, who would serve for a time in the Austrian parliament, also called for a unified German state. Schönerer was also a vehement anti-Semite who helped promote hatred of Jews among the German peoples. "We must thus insist unconditionally on the separating out of Jewish children and on the complete exclusion of Jewish instructors, whether baptized or not, from the schools of our race," Schönerer wrote in an essay on education in 1888. "Instead, we wish our youth to receive instruction and education according to Christian-Aryan principles."[7]

Social Darwinism

Schönerer and other writers and philosophers of the era adhered to other racist principles that helped form the basis of their insistence that Aryans were destined to rule the world. One of these principles is known as social Darwinism. Social Darwinism is a movement that found traction during the late 1800s and early 1900s. Its promoters borrowed the theory of evolution first suggested by British naturalist Charles Darwin in his 1859 book *On the Origin of Species*. In the book Darwin proposes that living things evolve over time and adapt to their environments in a process known as natural selection.

Darwin proposed natural selection as a biological theory, but others applied Darwin's principles to politics, suggesting that people who rise to the top of their professions—the wealthiest businessmen above all others—are the best qualified to govern nations. Schönerer and others took that interpretation of social Darwinism a step further, arguing that the German people held the responsibility for weeding out the ill, infirm, and handicapped from their society so that a master race would be bred and eventually take its place as world conquerors.

Hitler's Awakening

Absorbing these messages of German exceptionalism, anti-Semitism, and racial purity was a young Austrian, Adolf Hitler, who was born in 1889.

Social Darwinism

Social Darwinism would be embraced by the Nazis, who found it a viable strategy for cleansing the German population of undesirables. The theory was first promoted by Francis Galton, a cousin of Charles Darwin, in an 1869 book titled *Hereditary Genius*. In describing social Darwinism, Galton used the term *eugenics*, which derives from the Greek word *eu*, which means "good," and the suffix *-genes*. "We greatly want a brief word to express the science of improving stock . . . ," wrote Galton, "which, especially in the case of man, takes cognizance of all influences that tend in however a remote degree to give to the more suitable races or strains of blood a better chance of prevailing speedily over the less suitable than they otherwise would have had."

Under Galton's plan, the mentally and physical infirm would be medically sterilized and, therefore, unable to produce offspring. Eugenics found many proponents in Europe as well as America, among them author H.G. Wells, playwright George Bernard Shaw, and cereal company founder William Keith Kellogg.

In Germany the movement was promoted by physician Alfred Ploetz, who had published a book titled *The Competence of Our Race and the Preservation of the Weak* in 1895. In 1905 Ploetz founded the German Society of Racial Hygiene, which promoted social Darwinism. When Hitler was jailed following the Beer Hall Putsch, one of the books he is known to have read in prison was *Principles of Human Heredity and Race Hygiene* by Eugen Fischer, a well-known proponent of eugenics.

Quoted in Karl Pearson, *The Life, Letters, and Labours of Francis Galton,* vol. 2. Cambridge, UK: Cambridge University Press, 2011, p. 32.

A high school dropout, Hitler fancied himself an artist but was rejected for admission to the Vienna Academy of Fine Arts due to lack of talent. As a young adult he lived mostly in Vienna flophouses, holding many odd jobs—among them carpet cleaner, baggage carrier at a train station, and snow shoveler. Most of his meals were taken at charity soup kitchens.

To Hitler, it seemed his plight, and the plight of those in similar circumstances, would be improved through a unification of Austria with Germany and establishment of a strong German nation. Hitler also advocated elimination of Jews and other undesirables, who he believed were profiting off the labors of the downtrodden. He later would write in *Mein Kampf*, "The Jewish people, despite the intellectual powers with which they are apparently endowed, have not a culture—certainly not a culture of their own. The culture which the Jew enjoys today is the product of the work of others and this product is debased in the hands of the Jew."[8] Hitler held these beliefs even though his overcoat, the only garment that kept him warm during the frigid Vienna winters, had been given to him by a Jewish clothing merchant who had taken pity on him.

Wilhelm II and Weltpolitik

As Hitler continued to explore the ideas of Schönerer, Fichte, and other German nationalists, momentous events were taking place all around him. These events—developing in the capitals of Germany, Austria-Hungary, and other European nations—would have an enormous impact on Hitler's life as well as on the future of the entire European continent. In 1888 Wilhelm II, the son of a Prussian prince, ascended to power as the new kaiser. A firm believer in German exceptionalism, Wilhelm sought to extend Germany's borders across Europe. He had no need for the diplomacy of Bismarck, dismissing the prime minister in 1890. Wilhelm continued to oversee the industrialization and militarization of Germany and began making plans for expanded German influence in Europe and other continents.

By the late nineteenth century the British and French had both established colonial outposts in Africa, exploiting the country's rich natural resources to enhance their own wealth. They aimed to keep their colonies in Africa for themselves and were wary of German intentions.

In 1904 the British and French governments signed the Anglo-French *Entente* (agreement), essentially dividing up Africa between them.

Wilhelm had other ideas. In 1905 he visited Tangiers, Morocco—at the time a French colony—and declared his support for an independent Morocco. Wilhelm stopped short of pledging military aid to free Moroccans from French colonialism, but the message was clear to the French: Wilhelm aimed to become a player in international events. In 1897 Wilhelm appointed Bernhard von Bülow to serve as Germany's foreign minister. Bülow promoted a policy of *Weltpolitik*, or "world policy." In other words, Germany intended to influence world affairs. Says historian Hew Strachan, "This rested on the premise that the unification of Germany under Prussian leadership was not a culminating point in the history of the nation, but a new departure—a beginning, not an end."[9]

To pursue his *Weltpolitik*, Wilhelm believed he would need a strong military. For centuries the most powerful navy on Earth had belonged to the British. Wilhelm believed fervently in naval power and began funneling his country's resources into establishing a strong navy. By the early years of the twentieth century, Wilhelm believed his navy could challenge the sea power of the British. Germany's neighbors—the French, Russians, and others—grew wary of the kaiser's plans as they watched him build up his country's naval and land forces.

The Great War Erupts

Germany's fretful neighbors learned of Wilhelm's true intentions in 1914, when a cell of Serbian assassins murdered Archduke Franz Ferdinand, the heir to the Austria-Hungary monarchy. The Habsburg emperor, Franz Joseph, held dominion over territory in the Balkans that Serbia desired to absorb. Wilhelm saw the assassination as an opportunity for his Austrian ally to seize control of Serbia, which would extend German influence into the Balkans as well. He insisted to Franz Joseph that the Serbian government was complicit in the assassination (and, in fact, a nationalistic faction within the Serbian military had sponsored the assassins) and that Austria should respond by invading the Balkan nation. Wilhelm promised Germany would provide military support to the invasion.

An assassin shoots Archduke Franz Ferdinand in 1914, sparking the conflict that becomes known as World War I. Many countries viewed the war as an attempt by Germany to dominate the European continent.

On July 29, 1914, Austrian troops laid siege to the Serbian capital of Belgrade. The conflict would soon erupt into more than just a dispute between Serbia and Austria-Hungary. The Russians, who saw themselves as protectors of all Slavic peoples, sent troops to aid the Serbians. When the Russians entered the fighting, Wilhelm made good on his promise and sent German troops to Serbia.

Hitler's War Service

Soon after Germany entered the war against Serbia, Adolf Hitler enlisted in the German army's Sixteenth Bavarian Infantry Regiment. He initially served as a dispatch carrier, toting communications from commander to commander during battles. Hitler's unit received just three months of training, then was dispatched to the Battle of Ypres in Belgium, where the German army clashed with the British and sustained heavy losses. Hitler was one of the few members of the regiment to survive the battle. During four days of fighting, Hitler's regiment was reduced from a force of thirty-five hundred men to just six hundred.

Later, in October 1916 at the Battle of the Somme in France, Hitler sustained a wound to his leg. He received a promotion to corporal in March 1917. He was twice decorated for bravery, both times winning the Iron Cross—an esteemed award in the old Germany army. Accounts of how he won the decorations vary. It is said he captured fifteen enemy soldiers single-handedly, although official records of Hitler's battlefield feats do not specify the acts for which he was decorated.

Hitler's comrades found him hard to get along with. During moments between battles, Hitler would complain excessively about Jews, Communists, and others whom he loathed. Said one soldier who served with Hitler, "There was this white crow among us who didn't get along with us when we damned the war to hell."

Quoted in William L. Shirer, *The Rise and Fall of the Third Reich.* New York: Simon & Schuster, 1960, p. 30.

This conflict grew beyond a regional skirmish into a war that spread throughout the European continent and elsewhere as well. Dozens of countries joined the war, which they regarded chiefly as Germany's attempt to dominate the European continent through its own military as well as those of its allies, including the Austrians. The French, British, and, eventually, the Americans, would be drawn into the war. At the time it was known as the Great War, but decades later the conflict would assume the title of World War I.

An Enthusiastic Soldier

The war endured for four years, finally ending with the German people, economy, and military worn down by the fighting. The Germans suffered many battlefield losses, particularly in the last year of the war, after the Americans had joined the Allied cause. Within the ranks, the German army was afflicted with mutinies and desertions. Still, when the German troops marched home there was a strong belief among many of the vanquished soldiers that they had never really lost the war. Recalled one German officer, Carl Zuckmayer, "Starving, beaten, but with our weapons, we marched back home."[10] Instead, many Germans believed their leaders had given in to pressure exerted by German financiers and industrialists—many of them Jews—who feared financial ruin should the war continue.

One returning soldier who held that view was Hitler. By 1914 he had left Austria and was living in the German region of Bavaria. Hitler had grown hostile toward the large Slavic population of Vienna, which was now the capital of a sprawling empire that included Hungary. "I was repelled by the conglomeration of races which the capital showed me, repelled by this whole mixture of Czechs, Poles, Hungarians, Ruthenians, Serbs, and Croats, and everywhere the eternal mushroom of humanity—Jews, and more Jews," Hitler later wrote. "To me the giant city seemed the embodiment of racial desecration. . . . . The more I lived in this city the more my hatred grew for the foreign mixture of peoples which had begun to corrode this old site of German culture."[11]

Believing in the cause of German exceptionalism, Hitler enthusiastically joined the army and served with valor, twice winning decorations, twice sustaining wounds, and eventually winning promotion to the rank of corporal. As the war drew to a close, Hitler was sent home to recuperate from his wounds. At home, though, he found hostility toward the

German war effort by civilians who were weary of the conflict. Hitler regarded these complainers as slackers, and he later observed—to his way of thinking—that the loudest complainers were Jews.

Harsh Treaty Terms

On November 11, 1918, the German government signed the armistice (an agreement to end a war) and later agreed to the terms of the Treaty of Versailles, which stripped Germany of many territories, turning them over to the victors. Moreover, under the terms of the treaty, the Germans were forced to pay steep reparations to France, Belgium, and other countries that had suffered during four years of warfare. The financial penalties assessed on Germany under the Treaty of Versailles initially totaled $528 billion—a sum that would total nearly $1.5 trillion today. The treaty's harsh terms would help plunge postwar Germany into a deep economic depression, leading to widespread poverty, hunger, and homelessness. Returning home to Germany, Hitler resolved to enter politics and purge the German government of the turncoats who had agreed to the armistice and treaty. He also intended to begin the work of rebuilding Germany based on the principles of German nationalism, racial purity, and German exceptionalism that would soon become known as National Socialism.

Chapter 2

Chaos in Postwar Germany

Adolf Hitler returned home to Bavaria in November 1918 to find the local government in chaos and, much to his chagrin, a Jew in charge. His name was Kurt Eisner. In the final weeks of the war, Eisner had led an overthrow of the Bavarian duke, declaring Bavaria a democracy and independent of Germany. Eisner's independent state of Bavaria lasted less than one hundred days—he was assassinated by a German count who demanded restoration of the monarchy.

In the upheaval that followed, Communists took control of the government and declared Bavaria a Socialist republic. On May 1, 1919, the German army entered the Bavarian capital of Munich, massacred the Communists (about one hundred were killed in the shootout), and regained control of the Bavarian government. When the dust settled, an extreme right-wing government had taken office in Bavaria.

Such was life in Germany in the months following the armistice. In Berlin a new national government replaced the kaiser (who had fled to Holland at the conclusion of the war) and attempted to establish a democratic republic. Known as the Weimar Republic (named after the German city where the new German constitution was written), the new government faced tremendous problems. Anarchy was spreading through many German cities. Poverty, unemployment, hunger, and homelessness were widespread, and inflation was out of control.

Bloody Week

Among the groups seeking to gain power during this period of upheaval were the Communists, who attempted to seize authority throughout

Germany just as they had done in Bavaria. Indeed, in the months following the armistice, as the leaders of the Weimar Republic sought to bring stability to the country, they often found their efforts challenged by Communist organizations.

The Weimar leaders believed they had much to fear: in Russia Czar Nicholas II lost his throne in 1917 during a popular revolution. Following the czar's abdication, a democratic government lasted just eight months before it fell in a Bolshevik takeover. (The Communists in Russia adopted the name *Bolshevik*, a term that stems from a Russian word that means "majority.") As it had in Russia, the Communist movement was gaining popularity in Germany. In December 1918, just a month after the armistice, the first Soviet Congress of Germany met in Berlin and demanded the resignation of the Weimar leaders. The congress then moved to replace the government with a Communist regime in the mold of the Bolshevik government in the Soviet Union. Later that month a Communist cell in the German army broke into the headquarters of the Weimar government, cut the telephone lines, then took over the army's stables. (During the era, armies were still largely reliant on horses; therefore, the occupation of the army's stables by an enemy could have crippled the German military's ability to defend the Weimar government.)

The Weimar leaders were able to summon loyal forces within the army, and on January 10, 1919, a fierce battle was waged in Berlin between loyal German soldiers and the Communists within the ranks. The battle in the streets, which lasted seven days, became known as Bloody Week. It ended in a Communist defeat when the two top Communist leaders in Germany—Karl Liebknecht and Rosa Luxemburg—were captured and murdered by loyalist army officers.

The Communists were feared by proponents of democracy but also despised by the right-wing German nationalists. To their way of thinking, the Communists placed the rights of workers ahead of the priorities of the nation. Moreover, the Communist principle of equality for all working people, regardless of nationality, contradicted the notion of German exceptionalism. In *Mein Kampf*, Hitler denounced communism as a Jewish plot: "In . . . Bolshevism we ought to recognize the kind of attempt which is being made by the Jew in the twentieth century to secure dominion over the world."[12]

The leaders of Germany's Weimar Republic feared Communist influences during a period of extreme instability. The Bolshevik (Communist) takeover of Russia, sparked by the 1917 storming of the czar's winter palace (pictured), was seen as an ominous sign.

The German Workers' Party

At the conclusion of the war, Hitler elected to remain in the army. Although limited in size and arms by the Treaty of Versailles, the German army remained one of the few sources of steady employment in the country. Hitler was assigned to a Munich-based unit that investigated subversive organizations; in this role he was instructed to attend a meeting of the German Workers' Party.

The German government was wary of any organization that contained the term *workers*, fearing that it was dominated by Communists.

The Swastika

As propaganda chief for the National Socialist German Workers' Party, Adolf Hitler decided what the party lacked was a symbol. Hitler wanted a symbol with a stark and striking look—one that would immediately identify it as the insignia of the new Nazi movement. He chose the *hakenkreuz*, or "hooked cross," as the symbol. The Nazi symbol is more widely known as the swastika, a term derived from the ancient Indian word *svastika*, which means "good fortune." Indeed, the symbol of the hooked cross is believed to have been used as a sign of peace for some five thousand years before Hitler adopted it for the Nazi movement.

In the summer of 1920 Hitler, the one-time artist, designed the Nazi symbol as well as a flag for the party. On the banner, the black swastika appears in the center of a white disk, with the disk placed atop a red background. In *Mein Kampf*, Hitler explains the meaning of the Nazi symbol: "In red we see the social idea of the movement, in white the nationalistic idea, in the swastika the mission of the struggle for the victory of the Aryan man, and, by the same token, the victory of the idea of creative work, which as such always has been and always will be anti-Semitic."

Quoted in National Museum of American History, "The Price of Freedom: Americans at War," Smithsonian Institution, 2013. http://amhistory.si.edu.

While attending the meeting, Hitler concluded that the German Workers' Party was not dominated by Communists but rather by right-wing ideologues whose ideas about the future of Germany matched his own. At the meeting he met Anton Drexler, a Munich locksmith who had helped found the party. At the time it numbered no more than forty members. Drexler gave Hitler a pamphlet he had written that essentially laid out the principles of National Socialism: German exceptionalism, fierce nationalism, anticommunism, anti-Semitism, and racial purity.

Finding himself among friends and like-minded crusaders, Hitler elected to join the German Workers' Party.

At the time the party was composed of disillusioned, angry, and mostly unemployed Germans who continued to harbor a strong hatred toward their government for the loss in the Great War. "It was an organization with no assets except a cigar box in which to put contributions,"[13] says author Christopher Ailsby.

A Skilled Orator

As for Drexler, he found himself immediately suspicious of Hitler, describing him to a friend as "an absurd little man."[14] Despite Drexler's misgivings about Hitler, the newest member of the German Workers' Party made many new friends within the organization. Drexler appointed Hitler head of propaganda for the party—a post Hitler relished. As head of propaganda, it was Hitler's job to spread the party's message and help recruit new members. On one occasion, Hitler labored behind the keys of a typewriter, typing out eighty individual invitations to a party meeting. He then personally handed them out and was disappointed when only a handful of people showed up for the meeting.

He refused to be deterred. Hitler found the money to have the invitations mimeographed and then raised the funds he needed to place advertisements in a Munich newspaper, publicizing the party meetings. When more than one hundred people finally attended a meeting of the German Workers' Party, Hitler felt vindicated and confident that his efforts were paying off. "The success was positively amazing," Hitler wrote of the October 1919 meeting. "One hundred and eleven people were present."[15]

It was during this meeting that Hitler was given one of his first chances to address the group. Well before his rise to power, Hitler found that he was an effective speaker who could electrify groups with his oratory skills. "I spoke for thirty minutes," he recalled, "and what before I had simply felt within me, without any way knowing it, was now proved by reality: I could speak!"[16]

A Viable Political Party

Hitler poured all of his efforts into expanding the German Workers' Party, believing that it could grow into a viable political organization and eventually take over the government of Germany. Slowly, the party grew. By the end of 1919 the ranks had expanded to more than one hundred members.

Early in 1920 Hitler believed the party was ready to stage its first major event. He planned a rally for February 24 at the Hofbräuhaus, a beer hall in Munich with a seating capacity of more than two thousand. Hitler and other proponents of National Socialism spoke before a capacity audience. For some four hours, party leaders addressed enthusiastic crowd members, who gave standing ovations, cheered wildly, and embraced the message of National Socialism. At the conclusion of the rally, Hitler said, "I knew that now the principles of the movement which could no longer be forgotten were moving out among the German people."[17]

Soon after the Munich rally, Hitler resigned from the German army. He also convinced party leaders to change the name of the organization from the German Workers' Party to the National Socialist German Workers' Party. From that point forward, Hitler and his followers would be known as the Nazis.

Steps Toward Democracy

As Hitler worked in Bavaria to expand the reach of the Nazi Party, the leaders of the postwar government in Berlin were attempting to forge a democratic republic in postwar Germany. Democracy was a new concept to the German people, and many rebelled against its principles. The Weimar political leaders aimed above all else to maintain a peaceful transformation of government—instead of putting the kaiser on trial for leading the country into a disastrous war, they allowed the monarch to live in exile.

Indeed, the Weimar government intended to forge a democracy that would reflect the values of Great Britain, France, and the United States. The Weimar constitution, adopted on July 31, 1919, included a bill of rights guaranteeing all German citizens equality, free speech, free assembly, and other basic rights found in democratic societies. In the new constitution, representatives were elected to the national legislature by region, as they were in most Western democracies. The constitution also gave all citizens, including women, the right to vote (a right not granted to women in the United States until 1920). William L. Shirer comments, "It was . . . on paper, the most liberal and democratic document of its kind the twentieth century had seen, mechanically well-nigh perfect, full of ingenious and admirable devices which seemed to guarantee the working of an almost flawless society."[18]

Germans held their first national elections on January 19, 1919. In the weeks leading up to the election, street clashes broke out across Germany. Communists fought with advocates for democracy, most of them members of the Social Democratic Party (SDP), which held liberal democratic views and was emerging as Germany's most popular political party. Again, German Communists aimed to seize power. In the chaotic weeks leading up to the election, Germany's largest Communist party, the Independent Socialists, attempted to stage a coup; the revolt, however, was put down by the army.

Ebert's Popularity Is Tested

The January 1919 elections resulted in a victory for the SDP. The party was headed by Friedrich Ebert, a former tavern owner and supporter of trade unions. Ebert's party garnered 38 percent of the vote. Minor parties—which represented ideologies from socialism to monarchism—made up the rest of the vote. (The tiny German Workers' Party—not yet discovered by Hitler and at the time composed of no more than a handful of beer-hall malcontents and ruffians—was not a factor in the election.) The SDP formed a coalition with centrist parties soon after the vote, and Ebert was elected president of Germany's first republic.

Ebert's popularity was soon tested, as the decision fell on him to accept the terms of the Treaty of Versailles. Given Germany's weakened position, Ebert had no alternative but to agree to the harsh terms. Ebert's chief deputy during this era was Joseph Wirth, who held the office of chancellor. Wirth was leader of the Catholic Centre Party, which had garnered 20 percent of the vote in the 1919 election. Under the new German constitution, the president was the chief of state, but the chancellor was regarded as the top policy-making officer of the government.

Under the kaiser, the German government had financed the war by borrowing money from German banks. Following the war, the banks demanded payment on those loans. To pay these bills, as well as the reparations demanded by the treaty, Wirth instituted an economic policy that has often been practiced by governments facing tremendous financial burdens: he ordered the German treasury to print more cash. While this scheme usually helps solve immediate financial problems, in the long run it invariably causes inflation. Since the cash has little actual value to begin with, the more cash that is printed, the less it is able to buy.

Wheelbarrows of Worthless Cash

This policy caused widespread chaos. Germans found they literally had to walk into stores with wheelbarrows full of near-worthless German cash, known as marks, to buy milk, eggs, and other consumer products. But this runaway inflation and the virtual worthlessness of German money would have even more devastating effects: Germany planned to use this worthless money to pay its war reparations. The French soon had enough of this trick; on January 9, 1923, France sent troops into the Ruhr region of Germany and seized German coal mines. The French argued that if they could not receive their reparations in cash with real value, they would take it in coal.

The Weimar leaders in Berlin elected not to stage a military response to the French invasion. Instead, they called on German coal miners to go on strike, thereby denying the French the coal from German mines. The miners agreed, and the strike lasted for months. But the miners were now out of work and not collecting salaries; the German coal companies that owned the mines were also crippled. That September, the Weimar leaders asked the coal miners to return to work.

The anger over the French occupation of the Ruhr and the Weimar government's passive acceptance of the occupation led to widespread

President Friedrich Ebert (center) leads an inspection of the German military. Ebert's popularity was tested by his acceptance of the harsh terms of the Treaty of Versailles, which ended World War I.

public anger with Germany's elected leaders. Moreover, there seemed no end in sight to the runaway inflation and poverty that engulfed the German people.

"Hard as Steel"

No one held more contempt for Ebert, Wirth, and the other Weimar leaders than Hitler and his fellow Nazis. "If I ever come to power again there will be no pardons," declared Nazi leader Erich Ludendorff, a former army general. "With a good conscience I would have Ebert . . . and company strung up and dangling."[19]

By early 1920 Hitler was making plans to kick Drexler out of the party and to take command of the Nazis. Indeed, Hitler had little tolerance for Drexler, finding the intellectual founder of National Socialism confused and weak willed. "His whole being was weak and uncertain," Hitler said, "nor did he have the ability to use brutal means to overcome the opposition to a new idea inside the party. What was needed was one fleet as a greyhound, smooth as leather, and hard as steel."[20]

Adolf Hitler was able to gain control over the Nazi Party because he convinced wealthy Germans to contribute to the movement. Hitler, therefore, controlled the flow of cash to the Nazi Party. Without Hitler and the funds he was able to raise, party leaders knew their movement would die.

One of the first of these wealthy donors was Eduard Scharrer, the publisher of a Munich newspaper, who had met with Hitler in December 1922. During the meeting, Hitler had convinced Scharrer to contribute to the party after telling him that Communists (Reds)—and Jews—had infiltrated the Munich police. "The Reds are brilliantly organized," he told Scharrer. "The bulk of [police] officers are socialist, Red, Jewish."

During this meeting Hitler laid out his vision for a future Germany: he told Scharrer the country would rearm, then crush the homegrown Bolsheviks with an iron fist. After subduing communism in their own country, the Germans would attack the Soviet Union, exterminating the Russian people to make way for German expansion. He also pledged to eliminate Jews from German society.

Scharrer asked Hitler whether the Nazis were prepared to arm themselves to achieve their goals. "I hope we'll be getting weapons at the appropriate moment," Hitler replied. At the conclusion of the meeting, Scharrer donated 1 million marks to the Nazi Party.

Quoted in David Irving, "In a Secret Meeting at Munich's Regina Palast Hotel Hitler Sets Out His Secret Plans to a Wealthy Donor in December 1922, a Year Before His Ill-Fated Putsch," International Campaign for Real History, 2011. www.fpp.co.uk.

Hitler certainly saw himself in that mold, but another Nazi Party member also fit the profile of the type of man Hitler believed was necessary to propel the Nazis into power. His name was Ernst Röhm. He was a bull-necked former army captain whom Hitler found to be tough, ruthless, and driven. In fact, Röhm had played a role in putting down the Communist insurrection in Bavaria in 1918—leading his troops into Munich and overseeing the slaughter of the Communists. Later, when the Nazi Party organized its private army, the SA, Hitler placed Röhm in charge of this group of thugs.

The Führer

By 1921 Hitler's efforts to enlarge the Nazi Party began to pay dividends. By then he was recognized as the unofficial head of the party, a status he owed to the fact that he had personally recruited so many of its members, and now these allies had moved into influential party positions. Hitler was also responsible for attracting donors to the party; therefore, he controlled the flow of money into the Nazi Party.

Still, some factions remained loyal to Drexler and the other founders. In July 1921, while Hitler was away from Munich, a pro-Drexler faction of the Nazi Party proposed a merger with a right-wing group based in the city of Nuremberg. Their intention was to dilute Hitler's influence. Hitler learned of the move and hurried back to Munich to confront the insurgents. Convening a meeting of Nazi officials, Hitler threatened to resign if they pursued the merger. Realizing their party would lose the financial backing that Hitler had secured as well as his many followers, the insurgent party leaders agreed to drop their merger plans.

But Hitler now realized the moment was at hand when he could finally seize full control of the Nazi Party. He demanded that he be named *führer*, a German word meaning "leader," and be granted dictatorial power over the direction of the Nazi Party. Hitler's fellow Nazis sheepishly agreed, and from that moment forward there would never be another leader of the Nazi Party. As for Drexler, in later years the intellectual founder of National Socialism would be treated cordially by Hitler but he would never again hold power in the Nazi Party. Drexler lived out his life in poverty, dying in 1942.

Determined to Seize Power

By 1923 Hitler could now count some thirty-five thousand members of the Nazi Party; he had also formed the SA, placing the thuggish Röhm in charge. Hitler was emboldened by news that emerged from nearby Italy. A year earlier the Fascists under Benito Mussolini—whose policies closely paralleled those of the Nazis—seized power in Rome. Hitler concluded that it was time to make his push to seize control of Germany, starting the movement in Bavaria, where he planned to take over the local government.

That November he staged the Beer Hall Putsch, which failed and proved to Hitler that he had seriously overestimated the popularity of his own movement while underestimating the resolve of the Weimar government to maintain order. After spending nine months in jail, and authoring *Mein Kampf*, Hitler won his parole and stepped onto the Munich streets a free man. Jail had not deadened his spirit; he was as determined as ever to seize power in Germany. However, Hitler realized that the heavy-handed tactics that he had tried during the Beer Hall Putsch would fail, and that he would have to work through the democratic system established by the Weimar government in Berlin.

Chapter 3

The Birth of the Third Reich

When Adolf Hitler walked out of prison and prepared to return to rabble-rousing, he found the Weimar government had taken some steps to improve life for ordinary Germans. In 1924 the German foreign minister, Gustav Stresemann, had won concessions from the French that greatly reduced the reparations Germany was forced to pay under the Treaty of Versailles. Stresemann also had signed trade agreements with America that helped provide overseas trading partners for German industries and, therefore, foreign investment—and jobs—for German companies. Later, as chancellor, Stresemann had helped stem the runaway inflation by ordering the German government to stop printing money. And in 1925 he had convinced the French to leave the Ruhr. These achievements eventually earned Stresemann the Nobel Peace Prize.

Had the German economy and, therefore, the German standard of living continued to improve, it is possible that Hitler's movement would have died. His message of hate and insistence on targeting Jews, Slavs, and others as scapegoats may have fallen on deaf ears, saving tens of millions of lives as well as the destruction of much of the European continent.

Indeed, soon after leaving prison Hitler focused his efforts on recruiting new members, raising money, and establishing the Nazi Party as a political force. By 1928, though, it was evident that there was little enthusiasm among the German people for National Socialism. In that year's election, for the first time Nazi candidates ran for seats in the Reichstag. Nationally, the party polled less than 3 percent of the votes, and Nazi candidates won a mere 12 seats in the 491-seat legislature; in contrast, the SDP won 153 seats and remained in power. According to

Jeremy Noakes, an author and professor of history at Exeter University in Great Britain,

> The party's support was mainly limited to a few malcontents among the lower middle class—artisans and small retailers—but also a few extreme nationalists among the educated middle class: teachers, civil servants, doctors and ex-military men. By the beginning of 1928, it looked as though their enthusiasm would not be enough. . . . The party was exhausting the reservoir of the radical Right and the workers were not being converted.[21]

But thousands of miles away, events started unfolding that the Weimar leaders could not control. Soon, ordinary Germans would again find themselves victims of massive poverty, looking for scapegoats and finding comfort in the extremist ravings of the Nazis.

A Stateless Individual

The first blow to the future peace of Europe occurred on October 3, 1929, when Stresemann, again serving as foreign minister, died suddenly of a stroke. He was just fifty-one years old. In the hectic weeks that would follow, the Weimar government would miss Stresemann's intelligence, guile, and talent as a negotiator.

Three weeks after Stresemann's death, the American stock market crashed. Suddenly, the value of American corporations nosedived. Personal fortunes were lost overnight. Within a few months, the crash would lead to the Great Depression—an era of American history that saw massive unemployment, poverty, hunger, and homelessness. But as bad as it was in America, things were much worse in Europe, where industries relied on trade with American corporations. As American companies closed or greatly reduced their spending, their overseas trading partners felt the pain. And in countries whose economies still had not recovered completely from the Great War—Germany foremost among them—the Depression hit hardest of all.

All the while, Hitler continued to organize the Nazis, seeking believers in his movement. *Mein Kampf* was published in 1925, at first finding modest sales—it sold just 9,473 copies in its first printing. Indeed, following its introduction the book hardly sold at all—in the year before the American stock market crash, booksellers sold just 3,015 copies. But in 1930, after harsh times returned to Germany, people's interest in Nazism grew. This change was reflected in the sales of Hitler's book—that year *Mein Kampf* sold more than fifty-four thousand copies. By 1932 sales reached nearly one hundred thousand.

Hitler's success as an author may have been on the rise, but his influence as a politician was limited by a key facet of German law. Hitler, a native of Austria, believed in German supremacy. He called for the nation of Austria to be absorbed into Germany (the Habsburg monarch had been stripped of power under the Treaty of Versailles, and Austria-Hungary was split into separate nations). In 1925 he renounced his Austrian citizenship and considered himself a German. But the German

Members of the Hitler Youth salute during a speech by Hitler in 1937. The group indoctrinated young people into the tenets of National Socialism, creating a large and devoted following for Hitler and his party.

government did not accept his self-proclaimed citizenship; as a nonciti-zen, German law barred him from holding political office. Therefore, as Hitler worked to consolidate his power and build the Nazis into a viable political force, he was essentially a stateless individual.

Right-Wing Ideologies in the Reichstag

Despite this handicap, Hitler proved himself a keen organizer. At first, instead of attempting to win seats through elections, Hitler directed the party's efforts toward building support among citizens. The Nazis split Germany into districts, then assigned leaders to organize the par-ty in those districts, focusing on the establishment of Nazi-sponsored groups such as the Nazi Teachers' Association, Union of Nazi Lawyers, Order of German Women, and the Hitler Youth. The latter had the role of indoctrinating young people in the tenets of National Socialism. In 1924, as Hitler emerged from prison, he found that membership in his party had dropped to twenty-five thousand. By 1928 the organizational campaign had raised membership to more than one hundred thousand.

Despite the increased membership, the party made a dismal show-ing in the 1928 elections. Nonetheless, Hitler vowed to soldier on. The following year, as the Depression started affecting the German economy, the party's electoral successes improved. In local elections in northern Germany, where farmers were hit hard by the decline in crop prices, Nazi candidates received 10 percent of the vote—their best showing ever.

As the Weimar leaders in Berlin wrestled with the Depression, the liberal ideas espoused by Ebert and the Social Democrats were being replaced by right-wing ideologies. Ebert died in 1925; in that year's election, he was replaced by Paul von Hindenburg. The top-ranking German general during the Great War, Hindenburg was an enormously popular figure among the German people, but he was hardly a believer in democracy. Hindenburg's supporters hoped he would restore the monarchy in Germany. The former general never went that far, but there is no question that he disdained liberal politics, did not believe in government by the people, and hoped to eventually install a far-right system of governance in place of the Reichstag.

Nazi Propaganda

In the months leading up to the Reichstag fire, Adolf Hitler displayed the propagandist skills that he had honed a decade earlier. In simple terms, propaganda is misinformation masqueraded as news and disseminated to the public. Propaganda can be spread through paid advertisements, but throughout history propaganda has also been aired by news organizations that are aware of the mistruths but spread the lies because they are controlled by political or business leaders who believe in their mission.

Hitler's aim was to stir fear of Communists among the German people. He ordered Nazi-controlled newspapers to print exaggerated stories about the threat of communism while sympathetic radio commentators espoused Nazi doctrine as well. Across Germany, party members papered outside walls with posters warning of a Communist takeover of the government. In *Mein Kampf*, Hitler discusses his propaganda strategy:

> The receptive powers of the masses are very restricted, and their understanding is feeble. On the other hand, they quickly forget. Such being the case, all effective propaganda must be confined to a few bare essentials and those must be expressed as far as possible in stereotyped formulas. These slogans should be persistently repeated until the very last individual has come to grasp the idea that has been put forward.

Quoted in Roger Manvell and Heinrich Fraenkel, *Doctor Goebbels: His Life and Death*. New York: Skyhorse, 2010, e-book.

During Hindenburg's administration Stresemann negotiated yet another reduction in Germany's reparations under the Treaty of Versailles. Yet soon after the German economy collapsed, even this new payment scheme was too much for the German people to sustain. A group of wealthy Germans led by newspaper publisher Alfred Hugenberg began calling for total suspension of the Versailles reparations, arguing that the payments had been predicated on the assumption that Germany bore the entire responsibility for the war. Using his newspapers—he owned 150 throughout Germany—Hugenberg rallied support for this idea among his readers, finding particular traction for his position among Nazis.

Feeding Off the Discontent

The Nazis helped organize a referendum for the 1929 elections calling for suspension of the reparation payments. The measure garnered nearly 6 million votes, well short of the majority of 21 million the referendum needed for enactment. Nevertheless, the election results showed that the Nazis and their followers were gaining strength among the voters.

By 1930 the German economy was in a sharp tailspin; not since the years immediately following the Great War had so many people been without work, hungry, and homeless. Under the terms of the German constitution, Hindenburg held the power to employ extreme measures during times of national emergencies. To respond to the economic crisis, he appointed Heinrich Brüning as chancellor. Brüning shared Hindenburg's disdain for parliamentary government.

To avoid a return to inflation—in which the government would simply print more money to pay its bills—Brüning proposed a national budget that included severe cuts in social services. This budget, which would have subjected the poor, unemployed, and hungry of Germany to even more severe hardships, was rejected by the Reichstag. In response, Brüning convinced Hindenburg to schedule new parliamentary elections in September 1930.

This represented a golden opportunity for the Nazis. Feeding off the discontent of the German people, the Nazis garnered 6.4 million votes. Their candidates won 107 seats in the Reichstag, making the Nazi Party the second-largest bloc of votes in the legislature.

Hitler Is Appointed Chancellor

Nevertheless, the SDP still held the most seats and was able to govern with a centrist coalition. Brüning remained chancellor until 1932, when he was briefly replaced by Franz von Papen, an aristocrat who urged Hindenburg to appoint Nazis to ministerial positions. Hindenburg resisted: he was wary of the Nazis and harbored a particular disdain for Hitler. Hindenburg had been an officer and member of the military elite in the old Germany, and he still regarded Hitler as a lowly corporal, unintelligent, and little more than a beer-hall roughneck.

In 1932 Hindenburg faced reelection. By now Hitler felt he had achieved a measure of political power that would enable him to challenge the aging war hero. (The issue of his citizenship was quietly settled that year when a friendly government administrator appointed Hitler to a minor civil service job, which qualified him for German citizenship.)

For a country that had been making strides toward democracy, the 1932 elections for the presidency and seats in the Reichstag reflected the true chaos that resided below the surface. In the weeks leading up to the vote, street fights broke out throughout Germany. Dozens were killed by thugs, many of whom were SA toughs dispatched by the Nazis to ensure people voted for the National Socialism candidates. In the July election the Nazis polled nearly 14 million votes and won 230 seats—they now controlled the most seats in the parliament. Still, Hindenburg won the presidential election, defeating Hitler by some 6 million votes. In the aftermath of the election, with the Nazis now a major influence, Hindenburg nevertheless resisted demands by Hitler to cede power to the National Socialists.

And so, in December 1932, Hindenburg appointed Kurt von Schleicher as the new chancellor of Germany. Schleicher's tenure was short. He hoped to form a coalition government with elements from the left—particularly the trade unionists—as well as leaders from the right, including some Nazis he believed he could lure away from Hitler's control. He hoped to split the Nazis into factions to reduce their influence in the Reichstag. These efforts failed, and beginning in early January 1933, Hitler started meeting with Papen, the former chancellor who still held considerable influence over Hindenburg. Papen convinced Hindenburg to put his personal animosity toward Hitler aside, arguing that only Hitler enjoyed the political support of the Reichstag and the German voters to bring stability to the German economy.

On January 30, 1933, Hindenburg reluctantly agreed and appointed Hitler to the chancellorship. At one time destitute, living in flophouses and eating in soup kitchens, racist to the core, Hitler now held the second-highest position in the German government.

The Reichstag Fire

Hitler did not see the position of chancellor as the culmination of his political career—he aspired to greater heights. The Nazis still lacked an overall majority in the Reichstag; Hitler had no interest in forming a coalition government with centrists, who he knew would oppose his extremist policies. Soon after his appointment as chancellor, Hitler called for new parliamentary elections with the goal of winning a clear majority. New elections were scheduled for March 5.

In the weeks leading up to the election, Hitler and the Nazis threw a great scare into the German people, announcing that the Communists saw the coming election as their opportunity to take over the government. As a believer in German exceptionalism, Hitler had long despised the Communists and their principles of equality and workers' rights. And, by the early 1930s, he did have cause to be concerned that their message was resonating with the German people. In the 1930 election the German Communist Party had won 13 percent of the vote and seventy-seven seats in the Reichstag, providing the Communists with the third-largest bloc in the legislature after the Social Democrats and the Nazis. In the 1932 election the Communists increased their tally to 15 percent of the vote as well as the number of seats they controlled in the Reichstag to eighty-nine.

On February 24, 1933, Hitler's ally, Hermann Göring—a German air force officer during the Great War, now minister of the interior in Prussia—dispatched police to Communist party headquarters in Ber-

The Reichstag building, which housed the German parliament in Berlin, explodes into flames in 1933. The fire was orchestrated by Hitler but was blamed on the Communists.

lin. The Communists had long since abandoned the headquarters; by now, many German Communist leaders had either gone underground or fled the country. Nevertheless, Göring's police found crates of Communist party literature in the cellar. These pamphlets urged German workers to rise up and join a revolution against the German government. Hitler used the pamphlets and documents seized in the raid to alarm Germans, warning of a pending Communist revolt.

Evidently, Hitler concluded that the raid on Communist headquarters did not throw enough of a scare into German voters, and so he

The Death of the Reichstag

Adolf Hitler's assumption of dictatorial powers in 1933 ended the role of the Reichstag in German politics. Established in 1871 in the aftermath of the Franco-Prussian War, the Reichstag was sixty-two years old when Hitler ascended to power. However, for much of its existence the Reichstag was essentially powerless—first dominated by Otto von Bismarck and then by Wilhelm II. Only in the years after the Great War was the Reichstag truly the seat of a representative government in Germany.

By the early 1930s, though, little was being accomplished in the Reichstag. The legislative body was frozen by gridlock as extremists on the left (largely Communists) and those on the right (Nazis and other right-wing political leaders) blocked efforts to make new laws and solve the nation's problems. According to Georgetown University historian Walter Laqueur,

> There came a time, ten years perhaps, from 1919 to 1929, during which the German parliament did play a political role broadly comparable to that of the United States Congress. At the end of the decade, the antidemocratic parties on the left and right had a majority, and effectively prohibited parliamentary government. They also made the Reichstag a laughingstock; there were obscene interruptions, sessions had to be suspended. In the public mind the Reichstag became the *Schwatzbude*, the symbol for idle talk. The real decisions, the Nazis predicted, would be made in the streets.

Walter Laqueur, "The View from the Reichstag," *New Republic*, February 14, 1983, p. 14.

planned a much more sensational demonstration. On the night of February 27—one week before the election—the Reichstag building suddenly exploded in flames. Hindenburg, dining at his home with Papen (now the vice-chancellor), could see the flames from the dining room window. They quickly headed to the scene of the blaze, where they found Göring. "This is the beginning of the communist movement!" Göring declared. "We must not wait a minute. We will show no mercy. Every communist official must be shot, where he is found. Every communist deputy must this very night be strung up."[22]

The Enabling Act

A Dutch Communist and unemployed bricklayer, Marinus van der Lubbe, soon was identified as the culprit, although others were later arrested as part of a conspiracy. Van der Lubbe was eventually executed for the crime, although years later subsequent investigations revealed that he had confessed under torture and probably had been duped into helping to set the fire, which had been planned and ignited by Nazi thugs.

Hitler lost no time in seizing the opportunity presented by the Reichstag fire. He convinced Hindenburg to declare a state of emergency, granting the chancellor widespread and, to a large degree, dictatorial powers over the government of Germany. Hitler still planned to hold the elections on March 5. He sent Nazi thugs into the streets. They plastered buildings with Nazi propaganda posters and roughed up people they saw trying to tear them down. They set bonfires in parks and held rallies in which speakers denounced the Communist threat. Nevertheless, a clear majority again eluded the Nazis on election day— this time they garnered 44 percent of the vote. Still robbed of an outright majority in the Reichstag, Hitler resolved that he would not seek to govern by forming a coalition. Instead, Hitler intended to place the Nazis fully and completely in control of the German government.

On March 23 the Reichstag was scheduled to reconvene in temporary headquarters—the Kroll Opera House in Berlin. Earlier that day a minor branch of the German government, the Reichsrat (an upper house of the parliament, similar to the House of Lords in Great Britain) adopted the Enabling Act. This act gave the chancellor unbridled dictatorial powers. Under the terms of the German constitution, Hitler no longer needed to form a coalition in the Reichstag—he could rule as he pleased.

The Thousand-Year Reich

When members of the Reichstag took their seats that day, they found Nazi banners decorated with the symbol of the party—the swastika— draped throughout the opera house. When Otto Wells, the leader of the Social Democrats, stood in his seat to protest the powers granted to Hitler under the Enabling Act, the chancellor quickly took the podium and ordered him to be silent. "Your death knell has sounded," Hitler barked at Wells. "I do not want your votes. Germany will be free, but not through you!"[23]

For Germans, Hitler's assumption of dictatorial powers marked the beginning of what the Nazis called the Third Reich. (In German history, the First Reich is regarded as the Holy Roman Empire, which lasted from the tenth century to the early years of the nineteenth century; the Second Reich encompasses the reigns of Wilhelm I and Wilhelm II, which endured from 1871 to 1918.)

A year after assuming dictatorial control of the German government, Hitler predicted in an interview with *Time* magazine that the Third Reich would endure for one thousand years. He said, "At the risk of appearing to talk nonsense, I tell you that the Nazi movement will go on for 1,000 years! . . . Don't forget how people laughed at me, 15 years ago, when I declared that one day I would govern Germany. They laugh now, just as foolishly, when I declare that I shall remain in power!"[24]

Chapter 4

Intrigues, Expansion, and Appeasement

Soon after assuming the chancellorship, Adolf Hitler made it clear his ambition did not end with the ascension to power in Germany. To fulfill the principles of National Socialism, Hitler believed he would have to establish German exceptionalism throughout the European continent. That meant winning back territories given up by Germany under the Treaty of Versailles—and taking control of others.

Indeed, Hitler had dreams of pushing German borders 1,000 kilometers (621 mi) outward, extending far into Poland, Russia, Czechoslovakia, and other European nations. The Treaty of Versailles placed strict limitations on the size of the German army—limiting military membership to just one hundred thousand—but during the 1930s Hitler ignored the treaty and rebuilt the German military. He also imposed a draft, meaning all young German men were required to serve in their country's military. During their training, German soldiers marched to a song that included the lyrics, "We shall march on, for today Germany is ours; tomorrow the whole world!"[25] By the late 1930s the German military numbered nearly 3 million members.

Hitler's expansionist foreign policy, his dedication to rebuilding the German military, and his boasts of German exceptionalism raised concerns among the leaders of France, Great Britain, and other European nations. Throughout the 1930s, though, these countries employed a most unfortunate tactic when dealing with Hitler: they did nothing.

A Challenge from Röhm

Before fulfilling his dream of dominating the European continent, Hitler still had work to do to assure his rule at home. The leadership of the German army was wary of him, still not accepting the former lowly corporal as its commander in chief. He also found trouble in the SA, where his longtime ally Ernst Röhm was pressing him to incorporate the SA into the army. By this time the SA had grown to a membership of some 2 million. But German army officers were opposed to the incorporation of the SA members into their ranks, believing them to be unruly roughnecks unlikely to follow orders.

Hitler had long harbored concerns about the SA and its leader. Soon after taking over control of the Nazi Party, Hitler formed a division within the SA known as the Schutzstaffel (SS), which served as his personal bodyguard. (The word *schutzstaffel* means "defense echelon.") Hitler realized the value of an extremely loyal paramilitary force dedicated to his protection and soon started expanding the SS. He placed Heinrich Himmler, one of his most dedicated aides, in command of the SS.

Röhm also saw the SS growing in influence and aimed to remain in control of this division of the SA, which by early 1934 numbered some fifty thousand men. In February 1934 he conceived of a plan to win back the allegiance of the SS members. To the SA and SS members he considered most loyal, Röhm issued a dagger inscribed with these words: *"In herzlicher freundschaft Ernst Röhm"*—in English, "In cordial comradeship Ernst Röhm."[26]

Röhm awarded 136,000 daggers, including about 10,000 to SS members. Röhm knew the effect these daggers and their inscriptions would have on SA and SS members. To young German men of the era, loyalty to one's commander was foremost.

The Night of the Long Knives

Himmler had his own ambitions; he planned to oust Röhm and take over the SA. By the summer of 1934 unrest within the top echelons of the Third Reich had reached a boiling point. On June 21 Hitler

Members of the newly formed SS march in 1933. Originally created to protect Hitler, the SS developed into one of the most feared organizations in Nazi Germany.

met with President Hindenburg—by then ailing and confined to a wheelchair. Despite his infirmities, the intrigues involving the SA had reached Hindenburg's ear. The president told Hitler that unless he found a way to control Röhm, he would declare martial law. Under martial law, Hindenburg would place the army in charge of the government. At the time Hitler had still not won the allegiance of the army; therefore, imposition of martial law would certainly result in the ouster of Hitler from the chancellorship and an end to Nazi rule in Germany.

As for Röhm, the SA leader felt betrayed by Hitler and let it be known that his men would follow his orders—even staging a coup against the chancellor if he so commanded. Seeing an opportunity to rid the regime of his chief rival, Himmler told Hitler that Röhm had already authorized his men to take action against the chancellor—a story that Himmler is likely to have concocted.

The Death of Ernst Röhm

Ernst Röhm had been a valuable asset to Adolf Hitler during the early years of the Nazi movement, but by 1934 the head of the SA had turned into a major liability. As Hitler attempted to legitimize his authority, Röhm's SA troops were out of control—they were known to drive throughout the streets of German cities often drunk, abusing innocent citizens they encountered. Moreover, Röhm was homosexual. The Nazis had little tolerance for gays, believing their lifestyles were contrary to the principles of National Socialism and the establishment of a master race. As long as Hitler needed Röhm, he tolerated the SA chief's behavior, but Hitler found little use for the roughneck brawler after he had achieved the chancellorship.

When Hitler finally decided to rid himself of Röhm, he did it personally. On June 30, 1934, Hitler, accompanied by officers of the SS, arrived at a hotel in the German resort town of Bad Wiessee, where Röhm had convened a meeting of top SA leaders. Wielding a handgun, Hitler is said to have led the arrest of Röhm.

Röhm and other SA leaders were literally dragged out of their beds, thrown into cars, and taken to a nearby prison. In his cell, Röhm was handed a pistol containing one bullet in the chamber. The SA leader was told Hitler had decided to give him the opportunity to commit suicide. Röhm refused and was shot immediately by SS officers. His last words were reportedly, "*Mein führer! Mein führer!*"

Quoted in History Place, "Night of the Long Knives," 1996. www.historyplace.com.

Hitler chose to believe Himmler and decided to act, responding to all these threats against his rule with malevolence. On June 30, 1934, in an incident known as the Night of the Long Knives, Hitler ordered the arrests of Röhm as well as other SA leaders, several army commanders he suspected of duplicity, and various other political leaders with whom he was feuding. While held in their cells, Röhm and the others were murdered by the SS. In all, some four hundred leaders of the army, the SA, and political opposition groups were murdered.

Two of the army's most ardent opponents of Nazi rule—generals Kurt von Schleicher, who briefly served as chancellor in 1932, and Kurt von Bredow—were also killed that night. Schleicher and Bredow were not even arrested: they were both shot to death in their homes as they answered the knocks on their doors.

One political leader who met his death during the Night of the Long Knives was Gustav von Kahr, whose speech in Munich back in 1923 was interrupted by the Beer Hall Putsch. Kahr was able to thwart the Beer Hall Putsch by calling on loyalist soldiers to put down the Nazi threat, which resulted in Hitler's arrest and imprisonment. Hitler never forgave Kahr; after Kahr's arrest, Hitler had him shot along with the others. In a speech to the Reichstag following the Night of the Long Knives, Hitler said, "In this hour I was responsible for the fate of the German people, and thereby I become the supreme judge of the German people. I gave the order to shoot the ringleaders in this treason."[27]

An Oath to Hitler

After the Night of the Long Knives, Hitler disbanded the SA, merging its ranks into the SS with Himmler in command. The SS would go on to become one of the most feared organizations in Nazi Germany. The SS took on the role of a secret police force, acting above the law to purge German society of political adversaries and other troublemakers. The SS was also used by Hitler to further his goal of racial purity, using heavy-handed and violent tactics against Jews and others who would soon find their rights suppressed.

Hitler took other steps designed to consolidate his authority over the German people and the German army. He insisted that he be addressed not by his formal title—*chancellor*—but as *führer*. It was the same title Hitler assumed after taking over leadership of the Nazi Party, and its use was intended to send the message that he held absolute authoritarian power in the German government.

Moreover, he made all new army recruits swear an oath to God, making a personal declaration of allegiance to him. This was a significant command to the new recruits. In the German culture of the 1930s, personal oaths to God were taken to heart by citizens; after swearing those oaths, they were loath to break them. The oath also made it clear to all soldiers just who was in command of the army. The oath read, "I swear before God this sacred oath: I will render unconditional obedience to Adolf Hitler, the Führer of the German nation and people, Supreme Commander of the armed forces, and will be ready as a brave soldier to risk my life at any time for this oath."[28]

Seizing the Saar

Two months after Hitler's purge of the SA and the German army, the aging President Hindenburg died. Hitler demanded that the Reichstag merge the positions of chancellor and president—a measure that ran counter to the German constitution. To pressure the Reichstag, Hitler staged a public referendum on the question, easily polling 90 percent of the vote in favor of the merger. The Reichstag, now completely under Hitler's control, acceded to his wishes.

By 1935 Hitler felt the time had come to pursue German expansion beyond the country's borders. He looked first to a tiny region on Germany's western border, known as the Saar, which had been part of Germany before the Great War. Under the Treaty of Versailles the Saar had been made an autonomous territory, occupied by the French and British. Hitler wanted the Saar returned—mostly because of the region's rich coal deposits. In January people in the Saar voted overwhelmingly to be reunited with Germany; given the vote, the League of Nations felt compelled to ratify the transfer. (The league—a similar body to the United Nations—had been formed in the aftermath of the Great War; its purpose was to settle international disputes before they erupted into armed conflicts.)

Hitler looked next to another territory lost under the Treaty of Versailles. Known as the Sudetenland, the region had been part of Austria-Hungary prior to the Great War. After the breakup of Austria-Hungary the Sudetenland, which bordered Germany, was made part of Czechoslovakia. Its citizens spoke German, and Hitler demanded the Sudetenland be made part of Germany. During this era he was rebuilding German

SWEDEN

Memel ● LITHUANIA

DENMARK

Baltic Sea

North Sea

EAST PRUSSIA

Elbe

Berlin ●

NETHERLANDS

POLAND

GERMANY

BELGIUM

Rhine

LUXEMBOURG

Prague ●

CZECHOSLOVAKIA

Danube

Strasbourg ●

FRANCE

Vienna ●

AUSTRIA

HUNGARY

SWITZERLAND

ITALY

YUGOSLAVIA

- Germany
- Saarland, citizens vote to join Germany, 1935
- Rhineland, occupied and remilitarized by Germany, 1936
- Austria, annexed by Germany, 1938
- Sudetenland, annexed by Germany, September 1938
- Germany dismembers Czechoslovakia; creates protectorate of Bohemia and Moravia, March 1939
- Protective Zone created for German troops, March 1939
- Memel district, annexed by Germany, March 1939

industry as well as the German military. His efforts to modernize industry and rearm the military were virtually bankrupting the German treasury. Hitler knew Czechoslovakia contained ample raw materials, such as iron ore and coal, as well as many factories. And so while he called for the Sudeten Germans to be returned to the country of their heritage, he was far more interested in moving beyond the borders of the Sudetenland, occupying the entirety of Czechoslovakia and seizing its resources.

Apathy by the British and French

These designs did not go unnoticed by the other nations of Europe. In 1935 France, the Soviet Union, and Czechoslovakia signed a mutual defense agreement and made plans to build airfields in Czechoslovakia. Meanwhile, as Hitler eyed a push into Czechoslovakia, in 1936 he sent the Germany army into the Rhineland, a region to the west of Germany that borders Belgium. It was another territory lost under the Treaty of Versailles, and now Hitler demanded its return. Hitler had been told by his advisers to expect a military response from France and Great Britain, but much to his amazement, the two major military powers of western Europe made no protest.

Historian Oscar Pinkus says Hitler's intentions in occupying the Rhineland were clear: he was making plans for a new war. By moving an army of occupation into the Rhineland, Pinkus explains, Hitler established a formidable buffer that would have to be crossed by the French army. Indeed, if the French decided they could no longer tolerate Hitler's violations of the Treaty of Versailles, their army would have to fight its way through the Rhineland in order to invade Germany. Hitler did not believe the French had the stomach for what would prove to be a bloody confrontation. In fact, French leaders had no desire to provoke a military confrontation with Germany. At the time, the French government was besieged by its own problems—poverty, unemployment, and political unrest were widespread in France as well, and France's democratically elected leaders were proving themselves powerless to solve the nation's problems. Between 1932 and 1940 the French people elected sixteen different majorities to the country's legislature. Although the French signed a mutual defense agreement with the Czechs and Russians, Hitler felt strongly that if hostilities did escalate into warfare, the French would be loath to actually take up arms.

The British were also failing to realize the extent of the growing Nazi threat. Indeed, after the occupation of the Rhineland, many leaders of the British government felt the Nazis were justified in demanding return of the territory. As Pinkus asserts, "The reoccupation of the Rhineland was not seen as a milestone on the road to war, but as a rightful clamor of a people becoming master in its own house."[29]

The Bombing of Guernica

If it had not yet been clear to the British or French that Hitler was preparing for the next war, his actions in Spain should have sent a clear message. Hitler was anxious to see the effectiveness of the weaponry that had been produced by the German factories, and he would soon get his chance in Spain.

During the 1920s and 1930s Spain erupted into a hotbed of dissent as right-wing dictators, military leaders, Communists, loyalists to the Spanish monarchy, and advocates for democracy, known in Spain as Republicans, vied for power. In 1936 a fascist bloc under a military leader, General Francisco Franco, staged a revolt. For the next three years Spain would be engulfed in a bloody civil war that cost some four hundred thousand lives.

The Spanish Civil War also turned into a proxy war. The Soviet Union supplied arms to the Communists, who fought in a coalition alongside the Republicans, and Hitler and Mussolini provided arms to Franco's fascists. But Hitler did more than just send rifles and ammunition to Franco's soldiers; he used Spain as a testing ground for the weapons German industries were producing. On April 26, 1937, Hitler sent bombers to destroy the Spanish city of Guernica—a stronghold for Republican forces.

It was a Monday, market day in Guernica, meaning it was the day farmers brought their crops into the Guernica marketplace in the center of town. The town's population of five thousand swelled to ten thousand that day as people from surrounding towns shopped for food. As people gathered in the town square, the sky suddenly filled with the sounds of heavy engines. Above, bombers from the German air force— the Luftwaffe—filled the sky. The Luftwaffe's Condor Legion bombed the town for three hours, It is believed some seventeen hundred people were killed, and another nine hundred were wounded—providing Hitler with the proof he needed. His air force possessed devastating power.

The Invasion of Czechoslovakia

Knowing now that he possessed a fearsome military might, Hitler made his next move on Austria. He had always advocated that Austria should be absorbed into Germany; on February 12, 1938, he met with Austrian

The Nazi Salute

During the 1930s citizens of Germany were required to show their allegiance to Adolf Hitler by raising their arm in salute and shouting the phrase, "Heil Hitler!" ("Hail Hitler"). By the time Hitler became chancellor in 1933, dedicated Nazis had long been saluting their führer; now, though, as head of the German government, Hitler demanded that others salute him in that fashion as well. A 1934 decree ordered all civilian employees of the government to salute Hitler. Soon, many citizens of Germany had adopted the practice, and public displays of the Nazi salute were common.

In 1935 a German newspaper wrote,

> Our emerging task is to commit people to the majestic German greeting. . . . When we issue the German greeting as an expression of the state of our character to those who may still have doubts, we should be watchful that it is neither falsified nor deformed. These words of greeting . . . should continually raise us from the mundane details of everyday life and remind us of the grand goal and challenges Adolf Hitler has given us all. . . . This is a bit of practical National Socialism that everyone can perform.

> Moreover, at public rallies in which Hitler or other Nazi leaders were featured, the speakers would invariably shout, "*Sieg!,*" which means "Victory!" The crowd would then respond by answering with the shout of *"Heil!"*

Quoted in Tilman Allert, *The Hitler Salute: On the Meaning of a Gesture*. New York: Picador, 2009, e-book.

chancellor Kurt von Schuschnigg and demanded that Schuschnigg appoint Austrian Nazis into high government positions. When Schuschnigg refused, Hitler flew into a rage; he told the Austrian chancellor that unless he agreed to his demands, he would invade Austria. Realizing he had no choice, Schuschnigg reluctantly agreed. When he returned to Austria, however, he held a referendum asking the Austrian people whether they preferred an independent Austria or absorption by Germany. On March 12, shortly after the Austrians voted for independence, Hitler ordered his troops to cross into Austria. Schuschnigg and other Austrian leaders were arrested and thrown into prisons. Great Britain and France raised minor protests but again took no decisive action.

Finally, Hitler felt prepared to make his move on the Sudetenland and, eventually, all of Czechoslovakia. Hitler's propaganda chief, Joseph Goebbels, promoted the story that the German-speaking residents of the Sudetenland were facing abuse and discrimination by the Czechs. Inside Czechoslovakia, Nazi activists caused mayhem, staging a number of violent protests designed to show the Czechs that the Sudeten Germans favored German occupation. On September 1 Hitler ordered the German troops to mobilize on the Czech border. This time the British took a step toward diplomacy when British prime minister Neville Chamberlain traveled to Germany to meet with Hitler. During their meetings, Chamberlain again took the position that the Germans simply wanted to be reunited with their countrymen who lived across their border. Chamberlain found Hitler's demands reasonable and declared that Great Britain would not oppose a German occupation of the Sudetenland.

Not all British leaders were ready to agree to Hitler's demands. In Great Britain, Chamberlain's act of appeasement was loudly criticized by some members of the British parliament, led by Winston Churchill. As Chamberlain announced he had signed the Munich Pact, in which Great Britain agreed with Germany's right to occupy the Sudetenland, Churchill declared, "We have sustained a total, unmitigated defeat."[30]

On September 22, 1938, as Churchill and the others had predicted, German troops crossed the border into Czechoslovakia and then moved past the Sudetenland region, occupying the whole of Czechoslovakia. As the decade of the 1930s drew to a close, it became abundantly clear to Churchill and others that Hitler possessed a military capable of widespread destruction, and that further appeasement of the German leader would lead only to disaster.

Chapter 5

Holocaust and War

As Adolf Hitler expanded Germany's borders, he took steps to assure that dissent in his country was silenced. After taking office as chancellor, Hitler unleashed his pent up anti-Semitism against German Jews. Police were ordered to harass and arrest Jews. The first concentration camps were opened in 1933 and placed under the authority of the SS. In 1935 the German government imposed the so-called Nuremberg Laws, named after the German city where they were introduced during a Nazi Party rally. The Nuremberg Laws defined Jewishness, finding that Germans with at least two Jewish grandparents were, under law, Jews. Having defined just who was a Jew, the Nuremberg Laws stripped legally defined Jews of their rights as citizens.

Jews were not the only German citizens harassed and arrested: political opponents, Communists, and gays were rounded up and imprisoned. The Nazis aimed to rid their country of the Roma—then known as gypsies—and many were imprisoned as well. The Nazis also pursued their policy of eugenics, intending to purge their country of the handicapped and developmentally disabled, believing them to be burdens. These unfortunate citizens were also rounded up and shipped off to concentration camps.

To protest against the German government's treatment of Jews, Herschel Grynszpan, a German-born Jew who had fled to Paris, assassinated German diplomat Ernst vom Rath on November 7, 1938, while Rath visited France. The German propaganda machine declared that Grynszpan was part of a worldwide Jewish conspiracy to destroy the German state, stoking fears among the German people. On the night of November 9, Nazi thugs ran amok in the streets of Germany, Austria, and Czechoslovakia, vandalizing Jewish homes, Jewish-owned businesses, and synagogues. This sad chapter in German history is known as Kristallnacht, or the Night of Broken Glass.

For Jews, life in Germany and the German-occupied countries would only get worse. Jews soon lost their rights of citizenship. They were forced to wear patches bearing the six-pointed Jewish star on their sleeves, which identified them as Jews. In this manner, merchants, landlords, and others knew to refuse them service. Their homes, personal wealth, businesses, and other properties were seized.

Eventually Jews were arrested in massive numbers and sent off to concentration camps, where they faced starvation, slave labor, or certain death in gas chambers. Camps such as Buchenwald and Dachau in Germany, Theresienstadt in Czechoslovakia, and Auschwitz and Treblinka in Poland would earn infamous reputations as scenes of mass murder.

The Darkest Page of Human History

In Europe, it was the birth of the Holocaust, one of the darkest pages in human history. Some 6 million European Jews, as well as an estimated 5 million other enemies of the Nazi regime, were interned in concentration camps. Few would survive. According to Daniel Jonah Goldhagen, a professor of government and social studies at Harvard University, "During the Holocaust, Germans extinguished the lives of six million Jews and, had Germany not been defeated, would have annihilated millions more. The Holocaust was also the defining feature of German politics and political culture during the Nazi period, the most shocking event of the twentieth century, and the most difficult to understand in all of German history."[31]

Goldhagen and other historians wonder how a country of 80 million people could have wholeheartedly embraced Nazi racism and permitted the widespread slaughter of the Jews as well as the state-sanctioned theft of their property. Goldhagen suggests that the Nazis were expert propagandists, using their talents to convince ordinary Germans that Jews were the enemies of National Socialism. Indeed, in the years after Hitler ascended to the chancellorship, Jews were portrayed in the public media of the era—newspapers, newsreel films, animations, and outdoor advertising—as ugly, greedy, and heartless.

Nazi soldiers round up terrified Jewish families in the Warsaw Ghetto in 1943. Over the course of World War II, Hitler and the Nazis shipped millions of Jews to concentration camps where they were starved, tortured, or killed.

An Enemy Within Germany

It was necessary for the Nazis, Goldhagen says, to establish an enemy within Germany so the German people could be united in a common cause—to rid their country of undesirables. Moreover, Jews did not fit into the Aryan mold; therefore, under Nazi ideology there was no place for them in Germany's future. Slavs, Roma, gays, and others also did not fit the Aryan mold, and they fell victim to the Holocaust as well. In order for the Nazis to create the kind of world they envisioned, Goldhagen asserts, it became necessary to destroy an enemy so they could take credit for vanquishing a foe who stood between the German people and the utopian society that was their destiny to create. Goldhagen explains:

The Nazi German revolution sought to constitute and reshape the European social landscape according to its racial biological principles, by killing millions of people deemed, according to its racial fantasies, dangerous or expendable, and thereby to increase the proportion of the "superior races" and strengthen the overall biological stock of humanity and, complementing this, to reduce the danger to the "superior races" by the more numerous "inferior" ones.[32]

Himmler summed up the attitude when, in 1943, he declared: "Whether nations live in prosperity or starve to death interests me only insofar as we need them as slaves for our [culture], otherwise it is of no interest to me."[33] Historian Ian Kershaw adds that by the mid-1930s, Hitler had rescued the German economy from the Depression years. By the middle of the decade, the country was at full employment; homelessness, hunger, and poverty were now widely unknown in Germany. The fact that Hitler had rescued the German people from poverty by devoting much of their economy to producing weapons did not seem to matter much to them, Kershaw says, now that they had jobs and their pantries were stocked with food. Kershaw argues that when it came to the persecution of the Jews and others, ordinary Germans were willing to look the other way as long as the economy remained robust. According to Kershaw,

The view that Hitler brought order to Germany was one that persisted. . . . That despite "mistakes" (presumably those which had brought his country's ruination through war, and death and destruction to millions) he had "cleaned up" Germany, putting an end to disorder, stamping out criminality, making the streets safe to walk again at night, and improving moral standards.[34]

A Pact with the Soviets

During the late 1930s the German economy was centered largely on the production of weapons and bolstering the military. Although ordinary Germans were benefitting from the jobs created through the war industries, they were unaware that the military buildup was bankrupting their country. Despite Hitler's foreign policy initiatives—such as acquiring Czechoslovakia's raw materials and factories—the German government simply did not have the money to finance the country's militarization.

Hitler's ministers told him the government was barely able to pay its bills. Again, Hitler knew his dream of dominating the European continent could not be met without a strong military. To maintain that military, he would need a constant and dependable stream of raw materials as well as an industrial capacity to produce weapons. And so, in the next step of his plan to dominate Europe, Hitler eyed Poland.

The Polish border city of Danzig had a large native-German population. Again, Hitler's propagandists claimed the Danzig Germans were being abused by Poles. As the propaganda machine prepared Germans for an invasion of Poland, Hitler realized he would have to perform some delicate diplomacy with the one European leader he hated the most: Soviet leader Joseph Stalin.

Like Hitler, Stalin was a brutal dictator; but as a Communist and a Slav, the Russian leader was a natural enemy of all Nazis. Still, Stalin had his own designs on Europe, and they also included occupation of Poland as well as Finland, Romania, and the Baltic states. Therefore, on August 24, 1939, these two sworn enemies signed a nonaggression pact, essentially carving up Poland and agreeing not to go to war once Germany invaded.

By then, German troops had massed on the Polish border. On August 31, at 6:15 p.m., Hitler signed the order to invade Poland. At 4:45 a.m. the next morning, German troops crossed the border, touching off World War II.

This time France and Great Britain responded, mobilizing troops to come to the defense of the Poles. But their early mobilization efforts would fail—Germany's army, navy, and air force were too powerful for the outmanned and outmaneuvered French and British armies. In May 1940 British forces were pushed back to the coastal town of Dunkirk. From there they were forced to retreat from France with the help of merchant vessels and pleasure craft that made the daring rescue across the English Channel. On June 14, 1940, the German army occupied Paris.

The 1936 Berlin Olympics

The 1936 Olympics were staged in Berlin, Germany. Adolf Hitler hoped to use the Olympics as a showcase for German racial superiority, but his plans were thwarted by Jesse Owens, an African American and, therefore, a member of a race the Nazis regarded as inferior.

From August 1 through August 16, four thousand athletes from forty-nine countries competed in Berlin. Several weeks before the arrival of the athletes and the international press, the German government had ordered the removal of the "Jews not welcome here" signs and other anti-Semitic messages from the Berlin streets.

Germany's top athlete was Carl Luz Long, a long jumper whose blond hair and blue eyes helped define him as the textbook image of Aryan superiority. But Long was defeated in the long jump finals by Owens, who also won gold medals in the 100- and 200-meter sprints and the 4x100-meter relay. In fact, Owens broke eleven Olympic records during the games. He was one of ten African Americans on the US team, and among them they won seven gold medals, three silvers, and three bronzes.

When Owens defeated Long for the gold medal in the long jump, Long was the first to congratulate Owens. Hitler, however, refused to place the gold medal around Owens's neck. Two years later another African American helped disprove the notion of German exceptionalism. In 1938 heavyweight boxer Joe Louis knocked out German Max Schmeling in one round.

Hitler soon unleashed the Luftwaffe in attacks over Great Britain, bombing London relentlessly. And although the Royal Air Force responded with its own bombing campaign over Germany, the tide of the war did not change until 1943—more than a year after the Americans entered the conflict.

The Tripartite Pact

Relations between Germany and the United States had deteriorated throughout the 1930s. Although the Jewish community in America pressured President Franklin D. Roosevelt to come to the aid of European Jews, Congress was dominated by isolationist politicians who wanted no part of another European war. In 1935 Congress passed the Neutrality Act, which prohibited the United States from supplying arms to belligerent nations.

Still, Roosevelt attempted to apply diplomatic pressure to the European countries, urging them to find peaceful resolutions to their disputes. On April 14, 1939, he asked Hitler to promise that he would not invade his European neighbors. Hitler, however, turned the request into a humorous speech, drawing gales of laughter when he lampooned Roosevelt's appeal:

> Mr. Roosevelt demands that German troops shall not attack the following independent nations: Finland, Latvia, Lithuania, Estonia, Norway, Sweden, Denmark, Netherlands, Belgium, Great Britain, Ireland, France, Portugal, Spain, Switzerland, Liechtenstein, Luxembourg, Poland, Hungary, Romania, Yugoslavia, Russia, Bulgaria, Turkey, Iraq, Arabia, Syria, Palestine, Egypt.[35]

Hitler paused after reciting the name of each country, giving the crowd a chance to react with laughter.

As historian Robert Dallek explains, "In essence, [Roosevelt] was being told by Hitler, 'You're not a player in this world political game. We don't count you for very much, and we know that you've got a big political headache. Your isolationists are not going to let you do anything. You have all these neutrality laws. If we go to war against Britain and France, you're not going to have a significant say in things.'"[36]

In Asia, meanwhile, a Japanese military-led oligarchy had been pursuing expansionist plans that paralleled those of Hitler in Europe. When Japan invaded and occupied French Indochina in 1940, the United States and Great Britain enacted stiff economic embargoes that severely limited Japan's access to oil, iron ore, and other raw materials. Japan responded by establishing a military alliance with Germany and Italy. On September 27, 1940, the three countries signed the Tripartite Pact, establishing the Axis alliance. Under the pact, Germany, Italy, and Japan promised to come to one another's mutual defense in the event of an American attack.

Relations between Japan and the United States continued to deteriorate until the Japanese felt they had no choice but to strike against America. On December 7, 1941, the American naval base at Pearl Harbor in Hawaii was attacked by Japanese aircraft, resulting in the deaths of thirty-five hundred Americans.

America Enters the War

Four days after the Japanese attack, Germany declared war on America. The Japanese had not told Hitler that they intended to attack the American naval base; therefore, the assault on Pearl Harbor had taken the Germans by surprise. A day after the attack, the Japanese ambassador to Germany, Hiroshi Oshima, asked the German foreign minister, Joachim von Ribbentrop, to abide by the Tripartite Pact and declare war on America. Ribbentrop stalled, knowing Germany was under no obligation to come to Japan's defense since Japan had been the aggressor and, therefore, had not been attacked by the United States. Ribbentrop also feared that the US military's entry into the European war would lead to Germany's defeat.

But Hitler disagreed, believing that Japan would occupy America's military in the Pacific, and that Japan eventually would prevail. He hoped to enlist Japan as an ally against the Soviet Union. Hitler's non-aggression pact with Stalin collapsed in 1941, when Hitler ordered an invasion of the Soviet Union. So by the time of the Japanese attack on Pearl Harbor, Germany and the Soviet Union were at war.

On December 11, 1941, a German diplomat in Washington, DC, handed US secretary of state Cordell Hull a formal declaration of war. Later that day, in a speech to the Reichstag, Hitler drew a standing ovation when he attacked Roosevelt personally, accusing the American president of being a pawn of American Jews.

American troops go ashore on a beach in Normandy, France, on D-day. The landing was part of an Allied assault that forced Germany into fighting a two-front war.

Roosevelt responded with his own message, telling the American people that the Nazis represented a threat to world peace. "The forces endeavoring to enslave the entire world now are moving toward this hemisphere," Roosevelt said. "Never before has there been a greater challenge to life, liberty and civilization. Delay invites great danger. Rapid and united effort by all of the peoples of the world who are determined to remain free will insure a world victory of the forces of justice and righteousness over the forces of savagery and barbarism."[37] In Congress, the vote to wage war against Germany passed unanimously.

Nazis in Retreat

It took more than a year for the American military to mobilize, but in 1943 German dominance of the European continent showed its first cracks. Allied troops won decisive victories in North Africa, then launched an attack on Italy that quickly overran Germany's ally, deposed Mussolini, and knocked Italy out of the war.

The beginning of the end for the Nazi regime commenced on June 6, 1944. Known as D-day, some 160,000 members of twelve Allied armies took part in an invasion launched from Great Britain. The Allies crossed the English Channel, landing at beachheads in Normandy, France, where they overran the German defenders and began their push toward Germany. Paris was liberated by the Allies less than three months later. Hitler soon found himself fighting a two-front war: the Americans, British, and other Allied armies were approaching from the west, and the Soviets had the other half of his army pinned down on the eastern front.

The final German offensive occurred in late 1944 and early 1945. The German army attempted to drive back the Allied advance in the Ardennes, a region of Belgium, France, and Luxembourg. The offensive became known as the Battle of the Bulge because concentrated German forces were briefly able to push back the Allied lines, which formed a so-called bulge on the maps describing the conflict. The Allies nevertheless prevailed and defeated the German offensive. The battle exhausted the German military's ability to carry out the war; from that point on, the Nazi army was in retreat.

Hitler's Final Days

By the spring of 1945 the Germans were virtually out of food and ammunition. Young boys had been recruited to serve as soldiers because the German ranks had been decimated by battlefield deaths. Hitler's final days were spent in a bunker deep below his headquarters in Berlin. He had retreated there with a few top aides, their families, and his mistress, Eva Braun. Hitler and Braun married on April 29. In the early morning hours of April 30, Hitler was advised that Russian troops were overhead, searching for the bunker. Hitler realized his capture by the

During World War II Jews were rounded up and executed throughout Europe, but one place where they made a stand was in the city of Warsaw, Poland. Although herded into a walled-off ghetto, the Jews obtained smuggled guns. In January 1943 Jewish leaders learned the Nazis intended to clear out the ghetto, shipping some sixty thousand Jews to concentration camps. As Nazi soldiers entered the ghetto, they were fired on by armed Jews.

The Warsaw ghetto uprising proved to be more than just a temporary nuisance to the Nazis. The Jews fought bravely and were helped by circumstances in the war. At the time of the uprising, the Nazis were about to suffer defeat at the Battle of Stalingrad. Therefore, the German army was unable to devote its resources to a civil uprising in Poland. As such, the Germans were forced to retreat from the ghetto until soldiers could be diverted to Warsaw, which took until April 19.

As reinforcements arrived, German leaders thought it would take no longer than three days to put down the resistance; in fact, the Jews held out for four weeks. The Germans finally won the battle by setting fire to the ghetto. As the fire burned, the German commander, General Juergen Stroop, expressed surprise that the Jewish defenders would rather die in the fire than surrender. He wrote, "Despite the danger of being burned alive the Jews and bandits often preferred to return into the flames rather than risk being caught by us."

Quoted in William L. Shirer, *The Rise and Fall of the Third Reich*. New York: Simon & Schuster, 1960, p. 977.

Russians would mean he would be put on trial in Moscow, publicly humiliated, and then executed.

On April 30 Hitler and his bride ate lunch at 2:30 p.m. Shortly after their meal, the couple retired to their quarters. At about 3:30 p.m., gunshots were heard in the bunker. Rushing to Hitler's quarters, aides found the Nazi leader and his new bride dead of gunshot wounds to the head. Quietly, Hitler's aides removed the bodies from the bunker and burned them in a garden above the bunker while shells from the Russian army exploded in nearby streets.

The remaining German soldiers held out for another week. Finally, on May 8, 1945, the Allies declared VE Day—Victory in Europe Day. The rule of the Nazis had come to an end. The Third Reich, which Hitler had boasted would last one thousand years, collapsed after a mere twelve years.

Chapter 6

What Are the Legacies of the Nazis?

S ome 48 million people—members of the military, civilian noncombatants, and Holocaust victims—lost their lives during World War II. Citizens and soldiers from at least thirty nations were killed in the war. Soldiers died on battlefields. Sailors died when their ships were sunk by submarines or through air attacks. And Londoners died during the relentless attacks on the city by the Luftwaffe during what was known as the blitzkrieg, or "lightning war." Similarly, in February 1945 the German city of Dresden was bombed into virtual obliteration by Allied forces.

Nearly 10 percent of the war dead were Germans. Given that the prewar population of Germany stood at just under 80 million (including the German populations of Austria and the Sudetenland), it meant that about one in sixteen Germans lost their lives between 1939 and 1945. Given those numbers, it is conceivable that no German family emerged from the war without the loss of at least one member.

Long after the end of the war, the German people would continue to pay a heavy price for allowing themselves to be led by the Nazi regime. They soon found themselves pawns in the Cold War—the struggle between the United States and Soviet Union for influence in the world.

Four Zones

The rivalry between the United States and its allies and the Soviet Union would begin even before the downfall of the Nazis. In February 1945 Roosevelt, Stalin, and Churchill, who replaced Chamberlain as British prime minister in 1940, met to decide the fate of Germany. Meeting in the Soviet Union resort city of Yalta in February 1945, the "Big Three" world leaders discussed plans for the governance of Europe following the defeat of Germany.

At the conference in Yalta, as well as a subsequent conference in Potsdam in occupied Germany, it was decided that German territory would be returned to Poland, and that Germany would be divided into four zones; the Soviets, Americans, British, and French would each administer a zone. Plans were also discussed for completing the dismantling of Germany and creating a half-dozen or more independent states. Further, Germany's military would be dissolved, and all surviving Nazi leaders would be rounded up and tried for war crimes. Therefore, by 1945 the unified German nation forged by Otto von Bismarck was on the verge of collapse after just seventy-four years.

The Berlin Airlift

Although located in the Soviet zone, the agreement outlined that Berlin, Germany's largest city, would be divided into four sectors as well, with each of the four victors administering separate zones. It did not take long for friction to emerge among the victors. In 1948 Stalin attempted to seize control of the entire city by instituting a blockade of all railway and highway traffic into Berlin. At the time, Berlin—as with most of Germany—was destitute. The country's industries—which had done little for years but build weapons—had been virtually shut down. Once again, millions of Germans were out of work. Anxious to avoid a repeat of the post–World War I economy that drove the Germans into the hands of the Nazis, the Americans and other Allies had been propping up German society, supplying Germans with food and helping them rebuild their industries. "The best thing was the biscuit soup the Americans gave us," recalled Berliner Mercedes Wild. "You had a little food container. Maybe it had a lid, maybe it didn't. You filled it with food and you took it home for your family. Sometimes it was the only hot meal of the day."[38]

The blockade of Berlin would prove to be the first great test of the Cold War as Stalin intended to exert Soviet will throughout much of Eastern Europe. To overcome the blockade, the American and British air forces staged an airlift of food and other supplies into Berlin, flying over the Soviet roadblocks. For a year, the Western democracies delivered tons of food and other supplies to Berliners until, finally, Stalin concluded that the blockade had been ineffective and withdrew his troops from the railways and roadways.

The Birth of NATO

A year before Stalin had ordered the blockade, the American, British, and French governments agreed to combine the three German zones under their administration into a single zone. In 1949 the three Allies turned over governance of their zone to German political leaders, thus forming a new nation: the Federal Republic of Germany, known familiarly as West Germany. Stalin responded by nominally turning over administration of the Soviet zone to German political leaders as well. The new country, the German Democratic Republic, was known as East Germany.

As West Germany was given the opportunity to forge a free and democratic society, East Germany remained under the domination of the Soviets, who maintained control of a puppet government in Berlin, the East German capital. Despite being the capital of East Germany, Berlin remained a divided city with a free zone. Moreover, because the Western democracies regarded the Soviets as a threat to the peace of Europe, they elected to maintain a strong military presence in West Germany.

In 1949 the United States and several Western democracies formed a military alliance known as the North Atlantic Treaty Organization (NATO). (In addition to the United States, the other founding members were Great Britain, Canada, France, Denmark, Iceland, Italy, Norway, Portugal, Belgium, the Netherlands, and Luxembourg.) NATO was formed as a direct response to the growing power of the Soviet Union, whose postwar foreign policy closely resembled the type of aggression against weak neighbors that had been practiced by the Nazis. In 1948, for example, Communists seized control of the government

Barbed wire is reinforced along the Berlin Wall in 1961. The East German government erected the wall to separate the Communist half of Berlin from the free sector, and guards were ordered to shoot anyone trying to escape over the wall.

of Czechoslovakia, helped in no small part by covert aid provided by Stalin. Such Eastern European countries as Bulgaria, Romania, and Poland would soon be turned into client states of the Soviet Union as well.

NATO was formed to ensure Soviet aggression would not spread to Western Europe. Under the terms of NATO, an attack on one country is regarded as an attack on all members of NATO. Therefore, the entire and formidable firepower of NATO can be summoned to defend any one of its member nations. West Germany was permitted to join the alliance in 1952. By 2014 NATO had twenty-eight members, including Germany.

A Divided Country

The Soviet-backed puppet government of East Germany oversaw a Communist police state in which citizens enjoyed few freedoms. West

Nazis in America

According to the Southern Poverty Law Center of Montgomery, Alabama, an organization that tracks hate groups in America, there are at least 139 separate neo-Nazi groups in America. Most of these groups include individual chapters of national organizations with such names as the National Socialist Movement, the Creativity Movement, and the American Nazi Party.

These groups occasionally stage public rallies. Members of the National Socialist Movement are known to wear Nazi-style uniforms, including armbands that feature the swastika. Many of the groups espouse anti-Semitic rhetoric, but most seem focused now on blocking the expansion of immigration to the United States. Jeff Schoep, the leader of the National Socialist Movement, uttered a typical comment during an interview with a reporter in 2007: "When . . . you take a German Shepherd and mix him with a Golden Retriever you have a worthless animal that nobody wants and that isn't worth anything if you're trying to breed him or sell him. . . . These degenerates that allow their children to race mix and this sort of thing, they're destroying the bloodlines of both races."

It is difficult to estimate the number of active neo-Nazis in America. These groups generally do not keep records or, if they do, are unlikely to share them with journalists and others. In 2011 Schoep told the *New York Times* that his group alone includes a national membership of about four hundred members across thirty-two states.

Quoted in Southern Poverty Law Center, "National Socialist Movement," 2013. www.splcenter .org.

Germany, on the other hand, which was allied with the United States, embraced democratic reforms and built a strong economy. For decades, though, Germans lived in a divided country—with many family members unable to see one another because travel between the two Germanys was highly restricted.

In no part of Germany were tensions higher than in the city of Berlin. In 1961 the East Germans erected a wall in Berlin that separated the Communist half of the city from the free sector. East German guards were under orders to shoot citizens who tried to escape over the Berlin Wall.

For more than four decades NATO troops remained based in West Germany, where they were regarded as the first line of defense against Soviet aggression. By the 1980s nearly 2 million NATO troops were stationed in Europe, most based in West Germany. It was believed an equal number of Soviet troops were based directly across the border.

This standoff endured until 1990. With the Soviet Union in its death throes, the Soviet leadership in Moscow cut its ties to the East German leadership, withdrawing military and economic support for the Communist regime. The Communist leadership collapsed, opening the way for the reunification of Germany. The Berlin wall was torn down. Nevertheless, following the fall of the Third Reich, Germans were forced to live in a divided country for more than four decades.

Jews and the New Germany

Although Germany has rebuilt itself into a democratic and free nation, at least one group of people largely has been unwilling to accept Germany on its new terms: German Jewry has never recovered from the Holocaust. According to the advocacy group American-Israeli Cooperative Enterprise, the population of Jews in Germany in 2010 stood at about 120,000—one-fifth of the total number of Jews who lived in Germany in 1933, the year Hitler ascended to the chancellorship. Modern Jewish populations in other Nazi-occupied European countries have remained low as well. In Poland, the pre-war Jewish population stood at 3 million; in 2012, the Jewish population of Poland was reported at about 3,200 people. Nearly 1 million Jews lived in Romania prior to the war;

the 2012 population of Romanian Jews stood at fewer than 10,000. In the Netherlands, 160,000 Jews made that country their home prior to the Nazi occupation; in 2012, about 30,000 Jews lived there. And in Austria, where 250,000 Jews lived in the pre-war years, the American-Israeli Cooperative Enterprise reported a 2012 Jewish population of approximately 9,000 people.

Many Jews escaped from Germany and the other Nazi-occupied countries during the 1930s, establishing new homes in America and other democratic countries, but it is also true that many left behind family members who perished in the Holocaust. In America and elsewhere, many Jewish families can still recall memories of relatives lost in the concentration camps. The Holocaust has long preyed on the mind of American poet Rodger Kamenetz. Kamenetz has explained his relationship with Germany—one that is shared by many Jews—by recounting a 1990 stopover at the airport in Frankfurt, Germany, where he visited only briefly as he changed planes while traveling to India:

> On previous visits to Europe I had always avoided touching down on German soil. Now I knew why. Seeing German on posters put me on edge. So did the voices of German citizens around me. This was nothing I could help, an involuntary reaction, a stubborn prejudice.

> The mass of travelers surged into the main concourse and split up in all directions. I wandered around, hoping to bump into other members of my own party, who were arriving from New York, Boston, London, and Israel. We were all to meet at the New Delhi departure gate. Near a ticket counter, a man with a briefcase was berating a clerk. My ears pricked up at the sound of his voice. A few syllables of German spoken in anger and already the grainy newsreel was unwinding: Hitler, at a podium, the crowds at Munich, goose-stepping soldiers, the crowd responding with a massive Heil Hitler salute. And then, inevitably, the stacks and stacks of bodies. . . .

> But these businessmen and tourists hurrying through the concourse were not storm troopers, and it would have been

a stretch to imagine myself as a Jewish victim in striped pajamas. I am a grandchild of immigrants, Jews with the luck to get to America soon after the pogroms opened the long twentieth-century European Jew-killing season.

So I had no rational reason to feel uncomfortable in the Frankfurt airport. Surely these good German citizens would wish me no harm. Why hold a grudge against ghosts?

Yet . . . my discomfort was visceral. German poster. German language. German people made me nervous, and I wanted very much to find the other members of my group. I wanted to be with other Jews.[39]

The Birth of Israel

Following the war, many of the European Jews liberated from the concentration camps immigrated to the new state of Israel, created in 1948 by the United Nations. Over the six decades of Israel's existence, the Jewish population of the country has grown from those few thousand concentration camp survivors to a total of nearly 6 million.

The growth of the Israeli population can be attributed in no small measure to the relentlessness of the Israeli military, which has often been called on to protect the Israeli people from aggression by neighboring Arab states or Islamic terrorists who have vowed to destroy Israel. Certainly, the Israeli army finds a measure of its resolve in the Holocaust—vowing never to permit the Jewish people to face extermination again.

The Holocaust—in Hebrew, it is known by the term *Shoah,* meaning "catastrophe"—has greatly affected the course of modern Israeli politics. Contemporary leaders in Israel are loath to trust even their closest allies, including the Americans, and place most of their faith in the Israeli armed forces to protect the Jewish people. Many Israeli leaders wonder if this strategy can be sustained—that in order to survive as a nation, Israel will have to find ways to live in peace among its neighbors. "This national tragedy [the Holocaust] has become a de facto national strategy,"[40] says Avraham Burg, an author and former member of the Knesset, the Israeli parliament.

The Search for War Criminals

As Israelis struggle with their place in the twenty-first century, there are still efforts under way to bring those responsible for the Holocaust to justice. Even after nearly seventy years, former Nazis are still alive and hiding from prosecution.

In the first few months following the war, the Nazi leaders responsible for the Holocaust were tracked down and arrested; many were tried in 1945 and 1946 by military courts in the city of Nuremberg under the direction of the Allied victors. Most of the initial twenty-four defendants were sentenced to death penalties or lengthy prison sentences, some for life. Yet the search for Nazi war criminals did not end with Nuremberg. Over the years American and European prosecutors have brought cases against former Nazis who have been found in hiding. Even into the twenty-first century, as these former Nazis have reached their eighties and nineties, they have been discovered and ordered to face trial for war crimes in Germany. In 2013 the Associated Press reviewed government records and press reports and concluded that ten suspected Nazi war criminals—most of them former concentration camp guards or officers—were living in the United States, awaiting extradition to Germany for trial as their lawyers found ways to delay their deportations.

The Nazi Party has been outlawed in Germany, and the display of the swastika and other symbols of the Nazi era are prohibited under law. Nevertheless, the spirit of Nazism remains alive in many corners of the world. Right-wing and racist political organizations have emerged in some European countries, often as a response to the immigration of peoples from Middle East and Asian nations. In Greece, for example, the political party known as Golden Dawn has adopted a Nazi song, "Keep the Banner Flying," as its theme song. During World War II Greece was occupied by the Nazis, and some 160,000 Greeks lost their lives in the war, but those facts seem of little importance to party leaders who have found inspiration in the ways in which the Nazis sought racial purity.

Fringe Groups

The United States has seen its share of homegrown Nazis, known as neo-Nazis. In 1959 the American Nazi Party was founded by a white-

During a rally in Los Angeles, a white supremacist group flies its swastika flag and uses the Nazi salute. Groups such as this one perpetuate Hitler's hateful views in the United States and Europe.

power fanatic, George Lincoln Rockwell, who adopted the swastika as the party's emblem. Rockwell envisioned the party growing into an organization that could compete in American elections. In an effort to find a more widespread appeal, he eventually changed the name to the National Socialist White People's Party and dropped the swastika as an emblem. But his dreams of converting America into a state wed to the ideals of National Socialism died in 1967, when he was killed by an ex-follower whom he had kicked out of the party. The assassin shot the American Nazi leader as he walked out of a Virginia laundromat.

Today various hate groups have adopted Nazi symbols. Helped by the power of the Internet as well as the US Constitution's tolerance for free speech, they have remained active and able to spread their messages. Nevertheless, all of these groups remain fringe organizations as Americans have repeatedly rejected the type of rhetoric that so enthralled Germans in the 1920s and 1930s.

The Volkswagen Beetle

The familiar Volkswagen Beetle, which filled American streets during the 1960s and 1970s, was originally designed by Adolf Hitler in 1932. Hitler, the frustrated artist, made a sketch of the Beetle while sitting at a table in a Munich restaurant. He believed very strongly that all Germans should own cars, and he designed a compact car he believed would be affordable. He turned over the design to Jakob Werlin, the head of design at the German automaker Daimler-Benz, and instructed him to get busy. "Take it with you and speak with people who understand more about it than I do," Hitler admonished Werlin. "But don't forget it. I want to hear from you soon, about the technical details."

Daimler-Benz ultimately decided not to build the car. Eventually the design was turned over to engineer Ferdinand Porsche, head of the German automaker Volkswagen. (The name *Volkswagen* means "Car of the People.") But Hitler's car never went into widespread production during the prewar years at Volkswagen either. Following the war, a British army officer, Ivan Hirst, was assigned the task of restarting production at the Volkswagen plant. Hirst discovered the plans for the Beetle and realized the potential that an inexpensive car would have on the postwar world where, he was certain, everyone would want to own a car. The Beetle went into production, and models were soon exported to America and other countries.

Quoted in Hitler Historical Museum, "Adolf Hitler and Volkswagen," 1999. www.hitler.org.

The Germans themselves have acknowledged their responsibility for remembering the past. In 2013 German chancellor Angela Merkel laid a wreath at the site of the former Dachau concentration camp near Munich and met with some of the aging survivors of the camp. "Merkel is coming here to say we will never forget what happened here,"[41] said eighty-five-year-old Dachau survivor Abba Naor.

It seems unlikely that Hitler and the Nazis will soon, if ever, drop out of the public consciousness. The Nazis have left a legacy that will long be borne by the German people. This legacy not only will be studied by those who seek to understand and avoid a repetition of the world envisioned by the Nazis but also by those on the fringe who are strangely, and dangerously, drawn to the Nazi vision.

Source Notes

**Introduction: The Defining Characteristics
of Nazism's Rise**

1. Quoted in William L. Shirer, *The Rise and Fall of the Third Reich.* New York: Simon & Schuster, 1960, p. 69.

2. Shirer, *The Rise and Fall of the Third Reich*, p. 81.

3. Quoted in Richard Weikart, *Hitler's Ethic: The Nazi Pursuit of Evolutionary Progress.* New York: Palgrave Macmillan, 2009, p. 56.

4. Quoted in Weikart, *Hitler's Ethic*, p. 97.

5. Shirer, *The Rise and Fall of the Third Reich*, p. 82.

**Chapter One: What Conditions
Led to the Rise of the Nazis?**

6. Quoted in Lloyd Kramer, *Nationalism in Europe and America: Politics, Cultures, and Identities Since 1776.* Chapel Hill: University of North Carolina Press, 2011, p. 122.

7. Quoted in Werner Suppanz, "Georg Ritter von Schönerer," in *Antisemitism: A Historical Encyclopedia of Prejudice and Persecution*, ed. Richard S. Levy, vol. 1. Santa Barbara, CA: ABC-CLIO, 2005, p. 643.

8. Quoted in Adolf Hitler, *Mein Kampf: The 1939 Illustrated Edition*, trans. James Murphy. Berkshire, UK: Archive Media, 2011, p. 236.

9. Hew Strachan, *The First World War*. New York: Viking, 2003, p. 37.

10. Quoted in Michael E. Telzrow, "Lessons of the Weimar Republic," *New American*, May 11, 2009, p. 34.

11. Quoted in Shirer, *The Rise and Fall of the Third Reich*, p. 27.

Chapter Two: Chaos in Postwar Germany

12. Quoted in Hitler, *Mein Kampf,* p. 505.

13. Christopher Ailsby, *The Third Reich: Day by Day.* St. Paul, MN: Zenith, 2005, p. 9.

14. Quoted in Ailsby, *The Third Reich*, p. 9.

15. Quoted in Shirer, *The Rise and Fall of the Third Reich*, p. 39.

16. Quoted in Shirer, *The Rise and Fall of the Third Reich*, p. 40.

17. Quoted in Shirer, *The Rise and Fall of the Third Reich*, p. 40.

18. Shirer, *The Rise and Fall of the Third Reich*, p. 56.

19. Quoted in Nigel Jones, *A Brief History of the Birth of the Nazis.* London: Constable & Robinson, 2004, e-book.

20. Quoted in Ailsby, *The Third Reich*, p. 9.

Chapter Three: The Birth of the Third Reich

21. Jeremy Noakes, "The Rise of the Nazis," *History Today*, January 1983, pp. 9–10.

22. Quoted in Shirer, *The Rise and Fall of the Third Reich*, p. 192.

23. Quoted in Shirer, *The Rise and Fall of the Third Reich*, p. 199.

24. Quoted in *Time*, "Germany: Second Revolution," July 2, 1934. http://web.archive.org.

Chapter Four: Intrigues, Expansion, and Appeasement

25. Quoted in John George Stoessinger, *Why Nations Go to War*, 11th ed. Boston: Wadsworth, 2011, p. 56.

26. Quoted in Ailsby, *The Third Reich*, p. 54.

27. Quoted in Jewish Virtual Library, "The Night of Long Knives," American-Israeli Cooperative Enterprise, 2013. www.jewishvirtual library.org.

28. Quoted in Ailsby, *The Third Reich*, p. 56.

29. Oscar Pinkus, *The War Aims and Strategies of Adolf Hitler.* Jefferson, NC: McFarland, 2005, p. 23.

30. Quote in Shirer, *The Rise and Fall of the Third Reich*, p. 420.

Chapter Five: Holocaust and War

31. Daniel Jonah Goldhagen, *Hitler's Willing Executioners: Ordinary Germans and the Holocaust.* New York: Alfred A. Knopf, 1996, p. 4.

32. Goldhagen, *Hitler's Willing Executioners*, p. 448.

33. Quoted in Goldhagen, *Hitler's Willing Executioners*, p. 448.

34. Ian Kershaw, "The Führer Myth: How Hitler Won Over the German People," *Spiegel* Online, January 30, 2008. www.spiegel.de.

35. Quoted in *American Experience*, "FDR," PBS, 2006. www.pbs.org.

36. Quoted in *The American Experience*, "FDR."

37. Franklin D. Roosevelt, "Our Declaration of War," *New York Times*, December 12, 1941, p. 1.

Chapter Six: What Are the Legacies of the Nazis?

38. Quoted in *American Experience*, "Berlin Airlift," PBS, 2007. www.pbs.org.

39. Rodger Kamenetz, *The Jew in the Lotus*. New York: HarperCollins, 2007, e-book.

40. Quoted in Sandy Tolan, "Israel and the Psychology of 'Never Again,'" Salon.com, June 5, 2010. www.salon.com.

41. Quoted in Stephen Brown, "Merkel Pauses Election Campaign to Visit Dachau Concentration Camp," Reuters, August 20, 2013. www.reuters.com.

Heinrich Brüning: Appointed chancellor by President Paul von Hindenburg in 1930, Brüning responded to Germany's economic crisis by proposing a national budget that would severely reduce social services to Germans. In the parliamentary elections of that year, Germans responded to Brüning's austerity measures by electing 107 Nazis to seats in the Reichstag, giving the Nazis their first major electoral victory.

Bernhard von Bülow: Foreign minister under Kaiser Wilhelm I, it was Bülow who developed the policy of *Weltpolitik*—the principles under which Germany intended to become an influential member of the international community, exerting its will on its neighbors.

Neville Chamberlain: Prime minister of Great Britain in 1938, Chamberlain declined to oppose Adolf Hitler's demands to occupy the Sudetenland in Czechoslovakia. After meeting with Hitler, Chamberlain signed the Munich Pact, stating that Great Britain would not oppose the German occupation. His appeasement of Hitler was criticized at home, particularly by Winston Churchill.

Winston Churchill: When Churchill replaced Chamberlain as prime minister in 1940, Great Britain was already at war with Germany following the German invasion of Poland. Churchill ordered the bombing of German cities by the Royal Air Force and established Great Britain as a stalwart opponent of Nazism. He was instrumental in the negotiations that led to the governance of Europe in the post–World War II years.

Anton Drexler: Founder of the German Workers' Party, the Munich locksmith provided the intellectual timber on which National Socialism is based. After Hitler joined the party, he quickly pushed Drexler aside, finding the founder weak and incapable of resorting to the type of violent tactics Hitler was sure were needed to seize control of the German government. Drexler died in poverty in 1942.

Friedrich Ebert: The first president elected in post–World War I Germany, Ebert governed from the center. Although he was forced to agree to the harsh terms of the Treaty of Versailles, Ebert was able to steer Germany out of a dire economic depression.

Johann Gottlieb Fichte and Georg Ritter von Schönerer: The two nineteenth-century German writer-philosophers were among the first to espouse the principles of German nationalism, German exceptionalism, and institutionalized anti-Semitism. Their writings were studied closely by Hitler, who adopted them as the basic tenets of National Socialism.

Heinrich Himmler: As head of Hitler's private bodyguard, the SS, Himmler engineered the ouster of Ernst Röhm and would be charged with enforcing the Nazis' will on the German people. He was placed in charge of ferreting out political enemies, rounding up Jews and other undesirables, and ensuring the purity of the Aryan race. During the Nazi era he was personally responsible for millions of deaths.

Paul von Hindenburg: The top general in the German army during World War I, Hindenburg was elected president in 1925. He was wary of the Nazis and, despite their growing influence, declined to find places for them in his government. After defeating Hitler in the presidential election of 1932, Hindenburg reluctantly appointed Hitler chancellor the following year.

Adolf Hitler: Born in Austria in 1889, Hitler dropped out of high school and drifted through life until 1919, when he attended a meeting of the German Workers' Party and embraced the group's message of National Socialism. He would take over the party and ascend to the dictatorship of Germany, overseeing the murders of millions of people and plunging his nation into international warfare.

Ernst Röhm: The thuggish former army captain was an early believer in National Socialism and was placed in charge of the SA, a private army of roughnecks dispatched to silence critics. When Hitler suspected Röhm of planning to use the SA to stage a coup, he had the SA chief arrested and shot.

Franklin D. Roosevelt: President of the United States from 1933 until his death in 1945, Roosevelt was hindered by isolationists in Congress who prevented him from using more than just quiet diplomacy as the threat of Nazism grew in Europe. After Germany's declaration of war against the United States in 1941, Roosevelt oversaw the country's mobilization and participated in early talks on the governance of Europe following the war.

Joseph Stalin: Born Iosif Vissarionovich Dzhugashvili but known more familiarly as Joseph Stalin, he was a ruthless dictator who had his own designs on European domination. As a Slav and a Communist, he was a natural enemy of National Socialism; however, Hitler put aside his hatred for Stalin in 1939, when he signed a nonaggression pact with the Soviet leader enabling Germany to invade Poland. Hitler later broke the pact and invaded the Soviet Union, prompting Stalin to side with the Allies.

Gustav Stresemann: An effective chancellor and foreign minister during the years of the Weimar Republic, Stresemann won the Nobel Peace Prize for renegotiating the war reparations Germany was forced to pay under the Treaty of Versailles. Had he not died in 1929, it is likely Stresemann's talents could have helped rescue Germany from economic depression, thereby denying the Nazis the opportunity to exert their influence.

Wilhelm II: After ascending to the throne of the German empire in 1888, Wilhelm II aimed to make Germany a world power. A strong believer in German exceptionalism, Wilhelm modernized German industry and built up the German military. His desire to dominate the European continent plunged the European countries, and eventually America, into World War I.

For Further Research

Books

Anne Frank, *The Diary of a Young Girl*. Uttar Pradesh, India: Om Books International, 2013.

Uta Gerhardt and Thomas Karlauf, *The Night of Broken Glass: Eyewitness Accounts of Kristallnacht*. Cambridge, UK: Polity, 2012.

Brigitte Hamann, *Hitler's Vienna: A Portrait of the Tyrant as a Young Man*. New York: Tauris Parke, 2010.

Ian Kershaw, *Hitler: A Biography*. New York: Norton, 2010.

Margaret MacMillan, *The War That Ended Peace: The Road to 1914*. New York: Random House, 2013.

Adolf Hitler, *Mein Kampf: The 1939 Illustrated Edition*, trans. James Murphy." Berkshire, UK: Archive Media, 2011.

William L. Shirer, *The Rise and Fall of the Third Reich*. New York: Simon & Schuster, 2011.

Jonathan Steinberg, *Bismarck: A Life*. Oxford, UK: Oxford University Press, 2011.

Eric D. Weitz, *Weimar Germany: Promise and Tragedy*. Princeton, NJ: Princeton University Press, 2013.

Websites

Anne Frank House (www.annefrank.org). Anne Frank was a Jewish teenager whose family hid from the Nazis for two years in a secret room in a house in Amsterdam, Holland. After their discovery, the Franks were sent to concentration camps, where Anne died shortly before the end of the war. The diary she wrote while in hiding has been a best seller since its publication in 1952. The home where the Franks hid is now a museum; visitors to the museum's website will find many resources about Anne's ordeal and the Holocaust.

"The Berlin Airlift" (www.pbs.org/wgbh/amex/airlift). This companion webpage to PBS's *American Experience* series provides many resources about how the American and British militaries saved Berliners from starvation during the Soviet blockade of the city in 1948. Visitors can find newspaper articles reporting on the airlift, a map of Europe during the post–World War II era, and accounts of how American pilots delivered candy to Berlin children.

"Berlin 1936" (www.olympic.org/berlin-1936-summer-olympics). Maintained by the International Olympic Committee, this webpage chronicles the 1936 Olympics held in Berlin, Germany, in which Adolf Hitler intended to show off Aryan superiority. Instead, Jesse Owens and other African American athletes dominated the games. Visitors to the webpage can watch newsreel footage of Owens competing in the sprint and long jump competitions in which he won gold medals.

"Germany 1918–1939" (www.bbc.co.uk/schools/gcsebitesize/history /mwh/germany). Maintained by the BBC, this webpage provides many resources on life and politics in Germany between the wars. Among the topics that can be accessed by visitors are the Beer Hall Putsch, the economic problems facing the Weimar Republic, the Nazi beliefs in social Darwinism, the persecution of the Jews, the Reichstag fire, and the Enabling Act.

Jewish Virtual Library (www.jewishvirtuallibrary.org). Maintained by the American-Israeli Cooperative Enterprise, the Jewish Virtual Library contains many resources about Nazi Germany and the Holocaust. By following the link for the Holocaust, visitors can read about how Hitler rose to power, how he came to embrace National Socialism, and how he convinced the German people to accept his outlandish views.

National World War II Museum (www.nationalww2museum.org). Located in New Orleans, Louisiana, the museum chronicles the World War II era, highlighting America's participation in the international conflict. By accessing the "Explore WWII History" link, visitors can find resources on many topics, including the Holocaust, statistics on war casualties, a timeline of the war, and a glossary of terms used during the war years.

Simon Wiesenthal Center (www.wiesenthal.com). A concentration camp survivor, Simon Wiesenthal dedicated his life to tracking down escaped Nazis and exposing their crimes. The organization that bears his name administers Museums of Tolerance in New York, Los Angeles, and Jerusalem, where visitors can view exhibits dedicated to the Nazi era as well as other examples of prejudice against minority groups. Visitors to the organization's website can read about Wiesenthal's life and work.

Southern Poverty Law Center (www.splcenter.org). This advocacy group tracks hate groups in America and has chronicled the activities of neo-Nazis in forty-four states. The organization's website provides information on the activities of such groups as the National Socialist Movement, the Creativity Movement, and the American Nazi Party.

Index

Picture Credits

Cover: SA Brown shirts on parade, Reichsparteitag, Nuremberg, 1933 (photo), German Photographer (20th Century)/Private Collection/ Peter Newark Military Pictures/The Bridgeman Art Library

Maury Aaseng: 53

© Bettmann/Corbis: 31

© Stefano Bianchetti/Corbis: 19

© Heritage Images/Corbis: 25

© Hulton-Deutsch Collection/Corbis: 37, 60, 66

© The Print Collector/Corbis: 10

© Stapleton Collection/Corbis: 49

Thinkstock Images: 6, 7

© Richard Vogel/AP/Corbis: 79

© Vonderheid/dpa/Corbis: 73

Bismarck with Emperor Wilhelm I in a room in the Unter den Linden palace, Berlin (w/c on paper), Siemenroth, Konrad (1854–1915/16) (after)/Private Collection/The Bridgeman Art Library: 14

Reichstag fire, Berlin, 1933/Universal History Archive/UIG/The Bridgeman Art Library: 43

About the Author

Hal Marcovitz is a former newspaper reporter and columnist. He is the author of more than 150 books for young readers. His other titles in the Understanding World History series include *Ancient Rome, Ancient Greece, The Industrual Revolution,* and *The Arab Spring Uprising.*